GREAT CARS OF THE WORLD

Firsts in automotive engineering and design

GREAT CARS OF THE WORLD

Firsts in automotive engineering and design

JON PRESSNELL

PRION

First published in the United Kingdom 1992 by
PRION,
an imprint of Multimedia Books Limited,
32–34 Gordon House Road, London NW5 1LP

Reprinted 1993

Editor Nicholas Bevan,
Copy editor Raymond Kaye
Design Kelly j Maskall
Production Hugh Allan

A catalogue record for this book is available from
The British Library.

ISBN 1-85375-019-0

Printed in Italy by New Interlitho

Introduction

What makes a car great? The answers are in Great Cars of the World. I have charted the development of the motor car from Benz's frail tricycle of 1885 through to the sensational supercars of the 1990s, and have taken an enthralling look at the cars that have made history. It has been conceived and written from an international perspective ranging from such sporting greats as Bugatti and Ferrari which you will find alongside well-loved favourites such as the humble Austin Seven and the Model A Ford.

The engineering and design that has made these cars so special — whether talking of a utilitarian Citroën 2CV or a flamboyant coachbuilt Delahaye — is explained in detail. I have tried to guide the reader on an exciting voyage through a century of technical achievement and, with the help of award-winning photography, brought alive the designs that have led the world.

Jon Pressnell 1992

The classic Jaguar XK120. In 1952 it won the *Coupe d'Or* for its outstanding wins in the Alpine Rally.

How it started: Karl Benz's three-wheeler of 1885. This is in fact a replica built by Daimler-Benz and is in full working order: driving it is easier than you would think, at least on the level. The engine picture shows exposed crank, huge horizontal flywheel, belt transmission and simple differential.

The Birth of the Motor Car

At the end of the 19th century the car was only hesitantly beginning its evolution: other than its internal combustion engine, it had very little in common with the vehicles of today. Yet by the outbreak of the First World War in 1914, virtually every fundamental design feature of the modern motor car had been laid down — a bare 29 years on from Benz's first crude motorized tricycle.

The cars that led the way in this fascinating voyage of discovery are those that truly deserve the epithet 'great' — for without their inspirational example such progress would surely have been slower coming.

The pioneers: Daimler and Benz

The motor car has its origins in Europe, and more particularly in Germany, where Karl Benz (1844–1929) built his first petrol-powered tricycle in 1885. That same year Gottlieb Daimler (1834–1900) constructed a motor bicycle, and a motorized horse-carriage the following year.

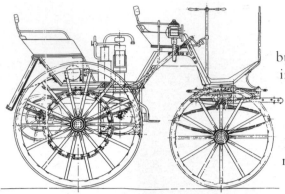

Others before them had built vehicles powered by the internal combustion engine. But Benz was the first person to offer for sale a workable motor car; and Daimler was the first to manufacture a purpose-built automotive engine.

Benz's three-wheeler of 1885 used a water-cooled engine seemingly based on a gas-powered stationary power unit. Horizontally mounted and with a huge horizontal flywheel and an exposed crank, it drove the rear wheels by belt and chain, through a simple differential. Advanced features were electric ignition and a mechanically operated rather than 'atmospheric' inlet valve.

In its initial form the Benz had a capacity of 985cc and was despairingly slow, so when manufacture began there was a larger 1.7-liter engine, and a two-speed transmission; power rose from an estimated ¾hp to around 2½hp. This was sufficient for a somewhat perilous 12mph (19km/h) maximum speed. Still, the Benz worked — as was proved many decades later by an 1888 example that successfully completed the celebrated London-to-Brighton Run at an average speed of 8mph (13km/h).

Production really got under way in 1890, and in 1893 came the first Benz four-wheeler. An adaptation of the original tricycle design, it was by that time distinctly old-fashioned. Despite being slow and unspeakably primitive, however, it was simple, relatively easy to maintain and repair, and gratifyingly durable. A twin-cylinder variant was latterly offered, but Benz's original designs continued largely unchanged, at his insistence. By 1901 the firm was in a mess.

Against Benz's wishes, a team of French engineers was recruited, who designed a new and up-to-date Benz. Introduced in 1903, it was not a success, and this caused Karl Benz to swallow his pride and come up with a modern four-cylinder in-line engine to fit in an adaptation of the new car's chassis; the company forged ahead as a result of this hybrid model.

Daimler got off to a slower start than Benz. More interested in stationary engines, he and his collaborator Wilhelm Maybach (1846–1929) made the first purpose-built Daimler car in 1889 and only began automobile production in 1895. In the meantime, however, the company had licensed its engines pretty widely, and so can take credit for launching such pioneer marques as the French Panhard and Peugeot.

The first Daimlers were primitive rear-engined devices with center-pivot steering, an unsprung rear axle, and a pulley transmission. Within three years, however, the firm had espoused a front engine, a leather cone clutch, and a gated gear change — not to mention a honeycomb radiator and proper Ackermann-type steering controlled by wheel rather than tiller.

A year later, in 1899, came a 24hp racer that developed these themes and was good for over 50mph (80.5km/h) from its thumping 5515cc four-cylinder engine. This Phoenix Daimler was high, cumbersome and potentially somewhat dangerous. Consequently one owner, the wealthy banker Emil Jellinek, felt moved to commission from the factory something lighter and more controllable and gave an undertaking that he would find owners for the first batch of cars. The outcome was the famous model named after his daughter Mercedes, introduced at the very end of 1900 and regarded by historians as the prototype of the modern car.

The 35hp Mercedes added to the gated gear change, honeycomb radiator and low-tension magneto ignition of previous Daimlers two crucial features: a low-slung lightweight chassis made of pressed steel, and mechanical actuation of the inlet valves. Initially this allowed the driver to vary the degree of opening of the valves, although this refinement was subsequently abandoned. This mix of ingredients resulted in a car with safer handling and greater engine responsiveness than had previously been achieved. Braking was impressive, too, and the superb drivability of the new model soon became a byword. Henceforth all these Daimlers would be known by the 'Mercedes' name.

France takes the technical initiative

We are, however, leaping ahead of ourselves. While in Germany Benz was stagnating and Daimler feeling its way steadily forward, the engineering initiative had in fact passed to France, and in particular to three great automotive pioneers.

Foremost among these was the firm of Panhard et Levassor, which specialized in bandsaws and woodworking machine tools. In 1890 it began production of the Daimler V-twin engine, and that same year built two horseless carriages powered by centrally mounted Daimler engines.

The following year a third vehicle emerged, with a vertically disposed engine mounted at the front — thereby enhancing stability by putting the weight of the engine over the steered wheels. The steering itself was to the Ackermann pattern, when others were still using the horse carriage system of center-pivot steering.

Less impressively, the clutch was a somewhat crude mechanism, and although the transmission used an advanced sliding-pinion arrangement, rather than belts, the gear clusters were ill-advisedly left exposed to the elements. Final drive was by a single chain, and there was only the most rudimentary of differentials.

But despite such conservative details, the 1891 Panhard established a mechanical configuration for the motor car that was to become near universal for 60 years or so: a front engine driving the rear wheels. In its first incarnation this *système Panhard* resulted in a harsh, difficult-to-drive car, compared to the smooth but pedestrian Benz, but there was the potential for infinite development.

This is what happened. Side chains and a bevel-gear differential came first, then a leather cone clutch as used on lathes and finally, in 1898, wheel steering operating a steering linkage and kingpin layout designed to give a degree of caster. This was the modern car in embryo.

Meanwhile the aristocrat Albert, Comte de Dion (1856–1946) had joined forces with the engineer Georges Bouton (1847–1938). After being involved at first with steam engines, in 1885 the firm of De Dion-Bouton made a crucial contribution to the development of the motor car. This was the manufacture of a modest ½hp engine.

Modest it might have been, but it was the first high-speed automobile engine, revving to 1500rpm and capable of 3000rpm without tearing itself apart. In contrast, a Daimler engine was restricted to around 700–900rpm. With its lighter reciprocating parts, accurate machining, and contact breaker coil ignition (necessary

The starting point — conventional Otto four-stroke engine of 1886. Heavy and bulky, it was hardly suited for automotive use, with its weight of 1456lb per horsepower; by contrast the Daimler engine was six times lighter.

Benz's first four-wheeler was introduced in 1892, and derivatives continued until 1901. Over 2300 were made, despite the car's primitive design. This is an 1893 Viktoria model.

to cope with the higher revs), this lightweight power unit decisively moved the petrol engine away from its gas and steam progenitors.

This mould-breaking engine was installed in a De Dion tricycle in 1895, and power was steadily increased from an initial ¾hp to a more potent 2¼hp. These trikes, cheap to buy, easily maintained and simple to control, enjoyed a considerable vogue, and firms were soon converting them to four-wheelers, with a passenger seat over the new front axle. De Dion-Bouton took the hint, and in 1899 offered a four-wheel *voiturette*, or 'little car'.

An improved 3½hp version on sale the following year featured the famed de Dion rear axle, a clever arrangement that reduced unsprung weight. It was not a novelty, for it had been used previously on steam carriages, and it probably was not invented by either de Dion or Bouton, but it was a means of rear axle location with many virtues: as the engineers at respected firms such as Lancia and Rover were to rediscover many years afterwards.

Despite subsequent two-cylinder and four-cylinder models, De Dion-Bouton's well-engineered little single-cylinder cars won the affection of many, and survived until 1912: they were reliable, comfortable, simple-to-drive, and adequately powerful. More to the point, however, the De Dion-Bouton engine was used in more than a hundred different makes of vehicle in the 1898–1908 period, and launched many a respected marque.

One such was the Renault, which had its own claim to fame. Louis Renault (1877–1944) was no engineering firebrand, but in his early years as a motor manufacturer he was not afraid of innovating. He demonstrated this to best effect with his 1¾hp car of 1898 with its tubular chassis, and powered by a De Dion engine.

This tiny vehicle did not only have a trend-setting direct-drive gearbox. It also transmitted power to the rear wheels not by chain but by a universally jointed longitudinal shaft, driving a live back axle by gears. In so doing it filled in the final piece in the puzzle, by laying down a pattern for a system of final drive that remains unchanged to this day — at least for those who continue to espouse rear-wheel drive. The propshaft had arrived, and chain drive would henceforth be on the way out. Admittedly this happened slowly — at the 1903 Paris motor show over 60 per cent of cars still used a chain-driven rear axle — but that should not detract from Renault's achievement.

Britain: from Lanchesters to Rolls-Royces

Britain lagged behind France and Germany in becoming a producer of motor cars; the first British-built Daimlers only emerged in 1897. Powered by Daimler engines initially imported from Germany, these were at first little more than adaptations of the Panhard et Levassor.

An appreciably greater achievement was the Lanchester, the idiosyncratic work of one of Britain's most lateral-thinking automotive engineers, Frederick William Lanchester (1868–1946).

The first Lanchester was built in 1895–6, but production only began in late 1900. In the words of historian Anthony Bird, it was 'the first motor car in the world to be scientifically designed as a complete entity'. Put another way, it resembled no other car of that time, or indeed of any other.

The power unit was a flat-twin with two counter-rotating crankshafts, each with three con-rods and connected through helical gears; the result was a balancing out of vibrations to give an engine of a smoothness unsurpassed at that time. Details included ingenious valve gear that ensured long valve life, and a fully automatic engine lubrication system. This extraordinary engine was mated to an epicyclic gearbox transmitting power to a worm-drive rear axle by means of a short propshaft. The axle itself had roller bearings and splined driveshafts, both

The first Mercedes of December 1900 was the forerunner of the modern car. Here it carries simple racing bodywork, for which a four-passenger touring body could be substituted. Clearly visible is the gated gear change.

Rather more conventional was the Napier, which in the early years of the century came to be regarded as Britain's foremost marque, and the one with the finest sporting reputation. In particular the company created what was arguably the first British racing car, in 1901, and won a notable victory in the 1902 Gordon Bennett race. It was also only narrowly pipped to the post by the Dutch firm Spyker (also spelled Spijker) in producing the first six-cylinder car. Unfortunately, in common with most early six-cylinder engines the Napier six suffered from marked crankshaft vibration. This was resolved, however, and the big Napiers became respected for their smoothness and easy flexibility, and for their pleasant gear changes.

The Napier, however, was comfortably eclipsed by one of the greatest cars of all time, the superlative Rolls-Royce 40/50 or Silver Ghost. Introduced in 1906, the six-cylinder 40/50 was the masterpiece of its designer, Henry Royce (1863–1933). Neither too large nor too costly, it offered refinement superior to any other car, thanks to the precision of its engineering and the exquisite standards of materials and assembly.

In the Silver Ghost you glided along in uncanny silence, at speeds of up to 70mph (more than 110km/h), yet at the same time enjoyed good roadholding and sharp steering. The mechanicals proved almost everlasting, and reliability — as demonstrated in some early publicity stunts — was equally legendary. So ahead of the competition was the Silver Ghost, indeed, that it remained in production until 1925, and only in its last years did it begin to show its age.

Unprecedentedly, too, the Rolls-Royce contrived to be regarded as the supreme luxury car of its era while at the same time retaining a sporting image. Partly this was because the car's proportions were so good that it managed to look dignified without seeming clumsy; partly it was due to sporting successes such as the Rolls-Royce team's dominant performance on the 1913 Alpine Trial.

In addition the Silver Ghost was judged by the British Army to be the

Preserved in a Paris museum, this 1891 Panhard et Levassor was the second car to be sold by the company, and was used for 40 years by its clergyman owner. With its engine mounted at the front, followed by the clutch and gearbox, the Panhard established the layout of the motor car for the next 70 years.

highly advanced features for the time.

All this was mounted in a rigid hull with items such as the fuel tank arranged to give additional bracing to the structure. Springing was by soft cantilevers, and light and positive tiller steering was used. Other features included clever low-tension magneto ignition, and a simple wick carburetor that avoided problems of dirt in the fuel.

Complex but logical, the twin-cylinder Lanchester was far in advance of its rivals, and offered impressive reliability, smoothness and ease of use. Alas, it arrived too late, just as the industry was standardizing on the simple and readily understood *système Panhard*. Subsequent Lanchesters remained unorthodox, but to a lesser degree. You can sometimes be too brave.

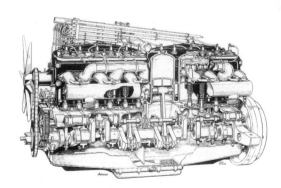

A masterpiece of British engineering — the 40/50 Silver Ghost power unit. Cylinder heads are non-detachable, there are seven main bearings, and lubrication is partly pressure-fed. The capacity is 7046cc.

De Dion-Bouton pioneered the lightweight high-speed car engine. Their single-cylinder *voiturettes* were simple, reliable, and very popular. This is a 1905 model with an 8hp engine.

most suitable chassis for its First World War armoured cars, and many such Rolls-Royces were still in service early in the following world conflict. Few high-class cars can have been so versatile.

Of course the Silver Ghost was not without its rivals, and foremost among these was the Tsar of Russia's favourite car, the French Delaunay-Belleville.

Advertised as 'The Car Magnificent', the Delaunay-Belleville was a beautifully made car from a firm specializing in steam engines: indeed, Queen Victoria's yacht had Delaunay boilers. From 1908 the company offered six-cylinder models of great refinement, with a notably rigid crankshaft (unlike some!), and it was one of the first manufacturers to use full-pressure engine lubrication.

While such vehicles as the Rolls-Royce and the Delaunay-Belleville were transporting the nobility in the manner to which they were accustomed, in Germany Daimler was building on the sporting reputation its 1901 Mercedes had so convincingly established.

Mercedes asserts itself

The Mercedes had made other cars seem old-fashioned, and Daimler pushed home its advantage with a 40hp model for 1902 and a thundering 9.2-liter 60hp Mercedes for 1903. After a factory fire had destroyed the super-powerful 90hp racers intended for the 1903 Gordon Bennett Trophy, the touring 60hp was substituted —

and carried off the prize. Good for over 80mph (130km/h) in stripped racing trim, or around 65mph (105km/h) with full touring coachwork, the Sixty was the supercar of its time. Even today, according to those who have driven one, the big Mercedes feels surprisingly manageable, with direct, responsive steering, a superb gear change, and an unusually quiet engine.

After a gap of a few years, Mercedes reasserted itself with a

Early British Daimlers copied Panhard designs, not always to good effect. Production began in 1897 and this model comes from that year; it uses a twin-cylinder engine.

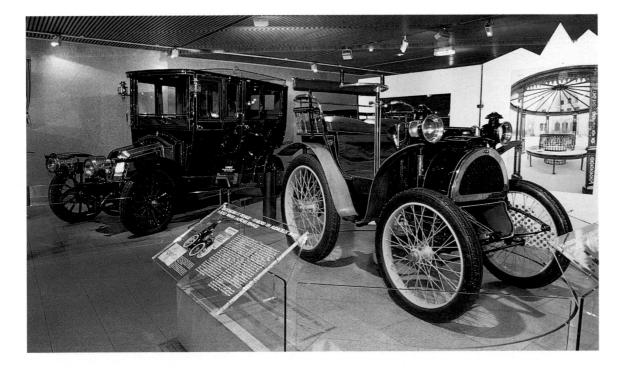

Louis Renault used a De Dion engine in his first cars and took drive to the rear wheels by a propshaft rather than by chain: a major innovation. The car shown is a reproduction 1899 car built by Renault. In the background is a 1907 Renault 14CV double *berline de voyage*.

combustion were improved by the 16 valves and the hemi-head.

Admittedly Henry had not got it quite right, as to realize the two latter benefits you really need a higher-revving engine than the Peugeot's. All the same, 148bhp at 2200rpm was not to be sniffed at, even from an engine as large as the original 16-valve car's 7.6-liter four.

The Peugeot was not slow in showing its prowess in competition, and its early victories included the 1912 GP and the 1913 Indianapolis 500. There was also a 3-liter version. For 1913 the 7.6-liter model was downsized to 5.6 liters and given a ball-bearing crank and a dry-sump lubrication system. In 1914 a new 4½-liter limit was introduced for GP cars, and that year's 4½-liter Peugeots featured a five-speed gearbox and four-wheel brakes.

In pioneering the 16-valve power unit the French firm deserves an important place in automotive history. The 1914 racers from the British firm Sunbeam were directly modelled on the Peugeot, as were the Tourist Trophy 16-valve Humbers of the same year, and soon the four-valve-per-cylinder layout was the norm for racing cars. Nor did the Peugeot's influence stop

Lanchester cars were highly unorthodox, but there was a strong logic behind the lateral thinking of their creator, Frederick Lanchester. This 1903 twin-cylinder has a mid-mounted engine and the raked front cowl typical of early Lanchesters.

victory in the 1908 French Grand Prix, using a 12.8-liter 135hp car purpose-built for the event. The days of such dinosaurs were drawing to a close, however, as new regulations sought to limit the capacity of GP cars.

Good-bye to brute force

This motorsport trend put the emphasis on advanced engineering rather than mere brute engine size, and brought to the fore the French marque of Peugeot. This came about as the result of Peugeot employing Swiss engineer Ernest Henry. For 1912 he and his team came up with something quite novel: a GP car with double overhead camshafts, four valves per cylinder, and hemispherical combustion chambers. Not only was valve actuation more efficient, but valve springs could be made lighter and thus less prone to breakage or to overstressing the valves, and breathing and

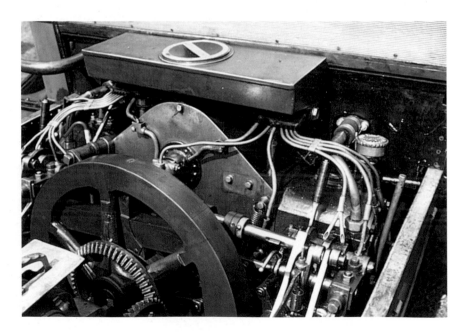

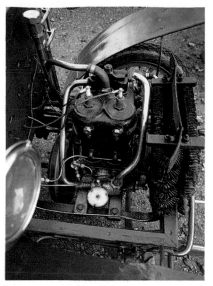

This 1903 Panhard is a well-known veteran of many London-to-Brighton Runs. It was owned by journalist John Bolster, and has a 1653cc twin. Maximum speed is around 32mph (52km/h), as power is only 7bhp.

there: the designer of the TT Humbers was one of W. O. Bentley's main collaborators, and a key feature of the 1919 Bentley was a Peugeot-inspired 16-valve cylinder head.

Thanks to manufacturers' participation in racing, these last few years before the First World War saw the evolution of a new type of car: the high-performance sports machine.

Proving that such a vehicle need not be a massively engined brute was one of the most significant cars of before the 1914 war: the modest little Type 13 Bugatti. Revolutionary at the time, this 1.3-liter *voiturette* of 1910 laid down the design markers for all Bugattis through to the last pre-Second World War GP car, the Type 59.

The approach chosen by Ettore Bugatti (1881–1947) was to use precision engineering to achieve mechanical efficiency and light weight. Thus the monobloc crankcase was in alloy and housed a ball-bearing crank, there was a single overhead camshaft, and gas flow in the head was carefully studied. The gearbox was compact, the chassis was light, and there was a novel multi-disc clutch.

The result was a lively car with a guaranteed 60mph (100km/h) capability and an extraordinary delicacy and ease of control: the engine was turbine-smooth, the gear change and clutch were deliciously light and did not demand double-declutching, and the car could be driven by the finger tips. And if anyone was disposed not to take this dinky little vehicle seriously, the makers were doubtless happy to point out that a Type 13 came second to a thumping great 10½-liter Fiat in the 1911 GP.

In Spain more traditional engineering was displayed by the four-cylinder Hispano-Suiza, but the well-handling Hispano that won the 1910 Coupe de l'Auto race evolved into the famous Alfonso of 1912, a 3.6-liter model with excellent road manners and a 70–75mph (112–120km/h) maximum speed.

Britain, meanwhile, fielded the 'Prince Henry' Vauxhall. Conservative but well-executed, this derived from a brace of 3-liter models that acquitted themselves notably well in the 1910 Prince Henry Trials in Germany. Elegantly bodied with a shapely pointed radiator, the 'Prince Henry' handled well and gave a strong performance: especially when it had been given a 4-liter engine.

Napier was one of the very earliest proponents of the six-cylinder engine. The car on the far right in this photograph is a 1910 4-liter model, silent and refined but with heavy steering (at least in this instance). Alongside is a 1904 Mercedes-Simplex, with a Rochet-Schneider of the same year visible through the screen of the car in the foreground.

This 1903 Mercedes 60 is actively used, not least in Vintage Sports Car Club trials: hence the incorrect rear tyres and the lack of mudguards. A similar car won the 1903 Gordon Bennett trophy. Engine is a 9236cc four-cylinder with overhead inlet valves and side exhaust valves.

Across the Atlantic, the very idea of such a sporting tourer was alien: in a country the size of the United States, with the roads in the state they were, the notion of touring was not on the agenda. Cutting a dash about town in a fast sporting two-seater was more the thing, and American manufacturers met this demand with various raceabouts. Among the best-known was the Mercer Raceabout.

With a body that was little more than a bonnet, a bulkhead, a couple of seats, and a bolster tank, the Mercer had a glorious stripped for action look, and a performance to match: it was guaranteed that the Raceabout would cover the mile in 51 seconds. The cars were not cheap, but that was because they were well engineered, with such details as a 44-plate oil bath clutch and vanadium steel road springs.

By the outbreak of the First World War the basic technological groundwork had been done. Overhead-cam engines, four-wheel brakes, independent front suspension, front-wheel drive and even four-wheel drive — all these had been tried, and in the United States Cadillac was in production with a V8 engine, and Packard was poised to launch a V12 in 1915.

The car as consumer object

The motor car was emerging from its childhood. It was also increasingly a consumer object rather than a mere aristocratic plaything: or at least that was how it was in the world's most important automobile market, the United States.

Oldsmobile had shown the way, with its famous and distinctly American Curved Dash lightweight buggy. First available in 1901, it was a clever exercise in minimal motoring. Long springs gave a comfortable ride on poor roads and a chug-along engine (maximum revs: 500rpm) and simple two-speed transmission made

the car easy, if slow, to drive. By 1903 annual production had reached 3000 cars, and two years later it had exceeded 5500.

Such exercises in the quantity production of basic transport paved the way for the legendary Model T of 1908, a car tailor-made by Henry Ford (1886–1947) for its intended role as a sturdy, simple and easy to drive vehicle.

The Ford's rugged large-displacement engine of 2.9 liters was deliberately restricted in its power output for the sake of durability, yet still gave 40mph (64km/h) and up to 27mpg. The chassis was light, but thanks to the use of high-quality vanadium steel it was also strong. The foot-operated two-speed epicyclic gearbox was unusual but largely idiot-proof. The rear axle was well located by a torque tube and had roller bearings for added durability. The engine, gearbox, clutch, transmission brake and propshaft universal joint housing formed a single unit.

All this added up to a seemingly indestructible, cheap-to-run

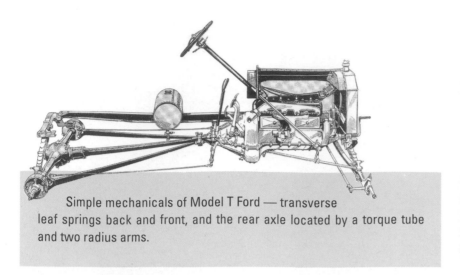

Simple mechanicals of Model T Ford — transverse leaf springs back and front, and the rear axle located by a torque tube and two radius arms.

The engine is a 7.4-liter six. Earlier Ghosts used a 7-liter unit.

car, with nothing fancy about it, but made of good quality materials. The steering of the Model T was a bit wayward, the brakes were poor, and the car had countless amusing and often aggravating quirks, especially in old age. No other car, however, put more novice motorists on the road, in more countries, over more years, than the Model T. And that makes the humble Ford a car of infinitely greater importance than any number of Rolls-Royces, Bugattis, and the like.

This Mercedes-Simplex is a 1904 example of one of the German Daimler firm's lesser models — it has a 5.3-liter four-cylinder engine with side valves. It surprises by its modernity even today.

More representative of coachwork on a Silver Ghost or more correctly a 40/50hp — is this four-seater touring body by Holmes of Derby. The car is a 1911 model.

This superb Rolls-Royce Silver Ghost is the original London-to-Edinburgh car of 1911, driven to the Scottish capital and back using only top gear. Average fuel consumption was 24.32mpg (11.6 liters per 100 km) , and the car's maximum speed, measured at the Brooklands track, was 78.26mph (125.9 km/h). The chassis is underslung, and the body is a specially built low-slung 'slipper' type.

The Bugatti Type 13 was a superbly engineered light car with a high-efficiency overhead-cam engine. It introduced many features that were to be seen on Bugatti cars right through to the 1930s.

The British firm of Maudslay was the first manufacturer to use an overhead camshaft — back in 1902. This 1910 32hp model also has a cross-flow cylinder head. Before making cars, Maudslay, of Coventry, built up a fine reputation as a producer of marine engines.

Peugeot's 16-valve competition cars brought a new efficiency to motor racing, and signalled the end of the might-is-right school of design. At first the engines were relatively large, at 7.6 liters, but a 3-liter version was soon introduced. Top Peugeot driver André Boillot is at the wheel of this example.

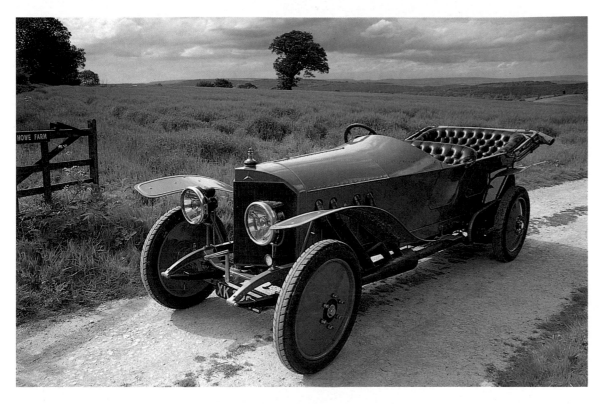

This Mercedes 37/90 is a 1911 model, chain-driven, and with a 9570cc overhead-valve four using two exhaust valves and one inlet valve per cylinder. This was the top Mercedes of the time.

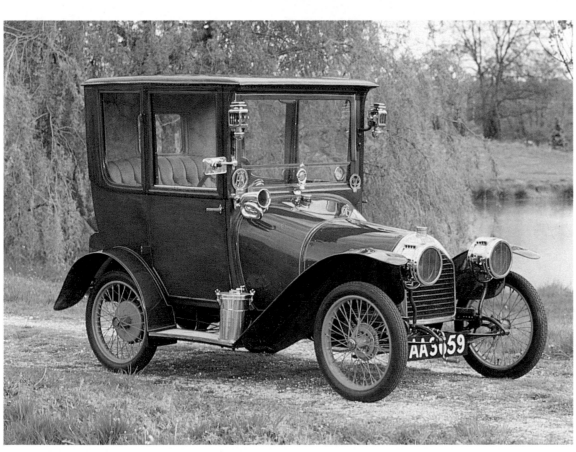

Another design by Ettore Bugatti was the Peugeot Bébé; over 3000 were made between 1913 and 1916. The little four-cylinder engine had a capacity of 850cc and developed 10bhp. Most cars had open coachwork, but a few had closed bodies, as here.

The Vauxhall Prince Henry was conservative but well-executed and led ultimately to the British firm's legendary 30/98 Vauxhall.

America's first sports car: the Type 35 Mercer Raceabout of 1910. The engine was a 5-liter T-head four with twin low-set camshafts and two plugs per cylinder, and a pressure-fed crank. Many American race successes enhanced the prestige of the car.

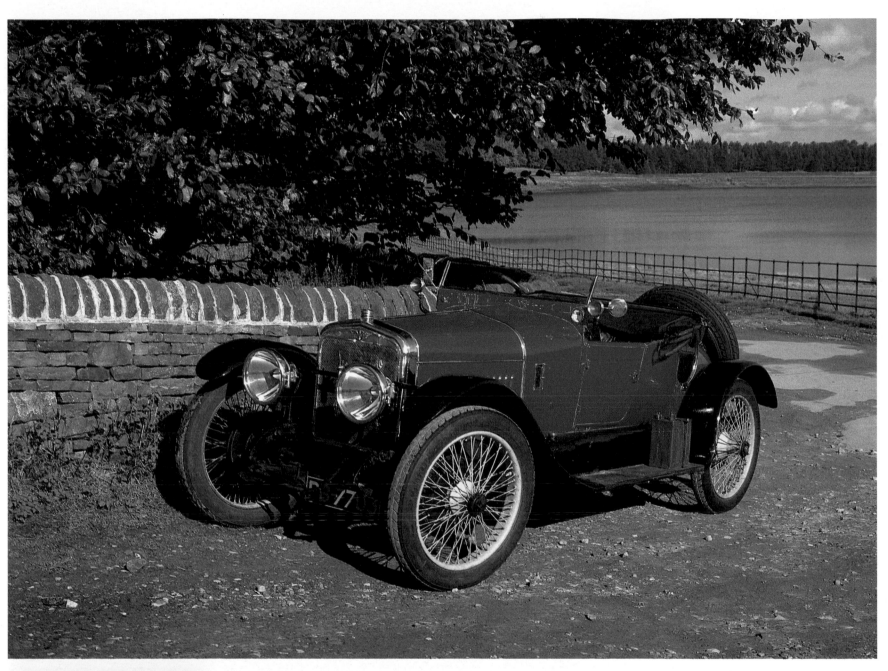

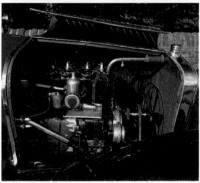

A delightful sports car of just before the First World War was the Hispano-Suiza Alfonso, a car that handled well, with a top speed of over 70mph (113km/h). This is a 1913 model from the Spanish firm; the SU carburetor is not a correct fitting on the 64bhp 3.6-liter T-head engine.

By the time this 30hp Daimler saloon was built, in 1913, the Coventry firm had established itself as one of Britain's foremost marques. It had also adopted the sleeve-valve engine, which gave the cars great smoothness at the cost of high oil consumption.

One of America's great success stories was the Oldsmobile Curved Dash. The single-cylinder engine has a capacity of 1 liter and a simple two-speed transmission is used. This is a 1903 model.

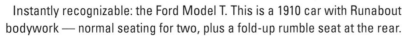
Instantly recognizable: the Ford Model T. This is a 1910 car with Runabout bodywork — normal seating for two, plus a fold-up rumble seat at the rear.

2

The Vintage Years

The years between 1919 and 1930 witnessed reputations made and manufacturing empires built that have lasted to this day. The period also saw the creation of some of the world's truly great cars.

Workhorses for the new motorists

Most significantly, and following the lead of Ford — who hung on too long with the Model T, but bounced back with the Model A — manufacturers developed low-cost, rugged workhorse vehicles for a new generation of motorist. For some of them, these cars became almost symbolic of their marque: in Britain Austin with the Seven, Morris with the Bullnose, and in France Citroën with the 5CV.

The Model A continued with Henry Ford's antiquated transverse leaf springing, but was otherwise a thoroughly orthodox machine. Power came from a sturdy, slogging 3285cc flathead four, and the new model offered the expected ruggedness along with an easy drivability.

A world apart from the Model A was the Austin Seven, one of Britain's most loved small cars. Announced in 1922, the Seven was a real car in miniature rather than a gimcrack concoction of motor cycle and motor car engineering. As such, it put paid to the countless quirky and unreliable cyclecars inflicted on Britain's minimal motorists, and it remained in production until 1939.

The Seven had a beautifully engineered but mechanically straightforward flathead four-cylinder engine, all but the first few of 747cc. This was mounted in a simple A-shaped frame, with a

transverse leaf spring at the apex to suspend the front axle and a quarter-elliptic spring tucked into each leg to locate the rear axle. All four wheels were braked, which was unusual for a light car of the period. The materials used in the Seven were of high quality and the lightness of the cheeky little 900lb (408kg) 'Chummy' open tourer gave the car respectable performance despite a power output of only 10bhp.

The Seven had a pitchy ride, an in-or-out clutch, questionable braking, and idiosyncratic roadholding, but its charm and its excellent standards of construction endeared it to generations of British motorists. It spawned various highly effective sporting derivatives, including a potent twin-cam racer, and in old age formed the basis of countless backyard specials.

The Citroën 5CV of 1921 was aimed at a not dissimilar market to the Seven's, but its appeal was much less wide — and much less durable. Following the 10CV models from André Citroën (1878–1935), which had pioneered mass production in France, the 5CV was a simple four-cylinder small car with quarter-elliptics

Ford Model A open two-seater with rumble seat: Gatsby-era glamour today, but in its time it was regarded as a simple and rugged workhorse. The A was current from 1927 until 1932, when it was facelifted and given a synchromesh gearbox to become the Model B.

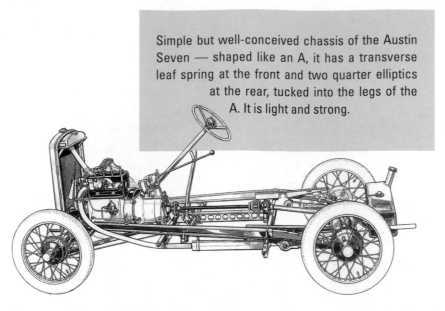

Simple but well-conceived chassis of the Austin Seven — shaped like an A, it has a transverse leaf spring at the front and two quarter elliptics at the rear, tucked into the legs of the A. It is light and strong.

Model A Ford sedan from 1928. After it had been facelifted in 1932 and became the Model B it was identifiable by its painted and more rounded radiator cowl.

front and rear and no front brakes, and was sturdily built to withstand France's poor rural roads.

Aimed at first-time motorists and — in a marketing first — at women drivers, the 5CV sold exceptionally well, but was discontinued in 1928. The little Citroën continued to serve French motorists well into the 1950s, however, and examples can still be bought for surprisingly modest sums.

The Morris Bullnose was no jokey miniature but a full-sized car, mass-produced in sufficient numbers for it to be sold at a rock-bottom price yet still be made to a high standard. First available in 1913, it lasted until 1926 and took Morris to a position of dominance in the British motor industry, with over half the market in 1929.

There were no mechanical surprises to the 1½-liter Morris Cowley or its sister model, the better-equipped, and latterly larger-engined Oxford. The Morris succeeded because of its price, and because it was simply engineered, built of high quality materials, and backed by a first-rate servicing network. It also had the virtue of being pleasing to the eye, thanks to its characteristic 'Bullnose' radiator.

The cars mentioned so far deserve their place in history for their crucial role in motorizing the public during the 1920s: their importance is primarily social and industrial.

The great British sports cars

Making a more emotional appeal are the great sports cars of the vintage era. Few come greater than Bentley, a marque whose achievements led to Britain becoming a dominant force in motor racing.

Captain Walter Owen Bentley MBE (1888–1971) announced the first car to bear his name in 1919. Intended as a reliable long-distance sports tourer with racing potential, the Bentley 3-liter had a 16-valve four-cylinder engine, as on the pre-First World War GP Peugeot and its imitators. It was soon active in competition, and in 1922 Bentley won the team prize in the Tourist Trophy race. A year later came a fourth place in the first Le Mans 24-hour Race, followed by a victory in the 1924 event. Further Le Mans victories in 1927, 1928, 1929 and 1930 established Bentley's reputation beyond all challenge.

Despite the evident sporting prowess of these machines, many purchasers saw the Bentley more as a powerful touring car, and thus opted for closed coachwork. In response, Bentley announced the six-cylinder 6½-liter model in 1925; two years later came an upgrading of the 3-liter, which became the famous 4½-liter. Then there was the Speed Six, a short-wheelbase tuned version of the 6½-liter that gave the best of both worlds, offering the sporting responses of the four-cylinder with the relaxed touring character of the six.

To many enthusiasts, however, the car that most symbolizes the vintage Bentley is the supercharged 4½-liter model. This is somewhat ironic, as it was only made in small numbers, it was built against W. O. Bentley's will, and it never won Le Mans. 'W. O.' favoured the Speed Six over the 'blower', and his instincts seem to

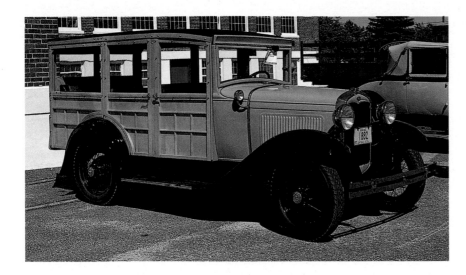

In 1929 Ford became the first manufacturer to offer a station wagon as a catalogued model, when it listed this Model A woody.

Sunbeam's 3-liter of 1925 was more technically innovative, as it was the first genuine production car to have double overhead camshafts. Steering, brakes and transmission were to the same high standard as this competition-derived power unit, but vintage experts judge the car again to have been let down by its chassis.

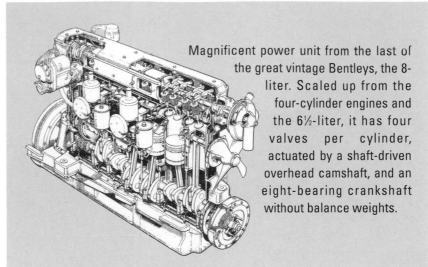

Magnificent power unit from the last of the great vintage Bentleys, the 8-liter. Scaled up from the four-cylinder engines and the 6½-liter, it has four valves per cylinder, actuated by a shaft-driven overhead camshaft, and an eight-bearing crankshaft without balance weights.

have been right, as the former model won the Le Mans 24-hour twice. Whether anyone should agree with the historian who called the supercharged 4½-liter 'the blown abomination' is another matter.

Bentley's final great achievement was the massive 8-liter of 1930, a car regarded by many as the ultimate statement of the British vintage era and its ethos. Both refined town carriage and 100mph (160km/h) grand tourer, it was aimed firmly at Rolls-Royce's Phantom II, and with development could have proved a superior car. Alas, the Depression caught up with Bentley, which went into liquidation in 1931 and ended up being bought by Rolls-Royce.

The other great British vintage sports-tourer of the period was the Vauxhall 30/98. First seen in 1913 as a 4½-liter development of the 4-liter Prince Henry model, it was very much Edwardian in concept, and more fast tourer than toned-down racer. Its big, flexible side-valve engine made it a top gear car rather than a raring-to-go sports car, and this character remained even after the 30/98 received overhead valves in 1923.

Enthusiasts will always dispute which is better, Bentley or Vauxhall, but the beefy and relaxed 30/98 could certainly show a straight 3-liter Bentley the way home, even if its whippy Edwardian chassis and indifferent brakes made its road behaviour less sure. This Vauxhall was current until 1927, and the last cars had hydraulic brakes.

To move down a notch, both Sunbeam and Lagonda offered much respected sporting cars in the 1920s. In 1925 Lagonda came out with a 2-liter with twin high-set (not overhead) camshafts, and from 1927 a sports version was offered. Unfortunately a heavy chassis blunted performance.

A gathering of Austin Sevens. Front left is a 1936 Nippy sports model; front right an unsupercharged Ulster; centre a 1928 'Chummy'. Back row left to right a 1928–9 'Top Hat' saloon; a 1938 Ruby; a 1934 Box saloon; a 1930 American-built Bantam roadster.

Altogether different was the Frazer Nash, another car at the top of the desirability tree for vintage enthusiasts in Britain. Evolved from the GN sporting cycle car, it was an uncompromising sports car, light and simple to the point of crudity. Its key feature, inherited from the GN, was differential-less final drive by chain and sprocket.

Fast, highly manoeuvrable and with an instant gear change, it stood in a class alone: especially when it received an ohv Meadows engine and a four-speed gearbox in 1929. Frazer Nash sporting successes were many, and the marque's reputation stands far higher than a production run of only 380 or so cars might lead you to expect. The Frazer Nash, however, was an expensive car, out of reach of the average enthusiast. Perhaps such a driver would plump instead for a sports model Austin Seven, but from 1929 he had another

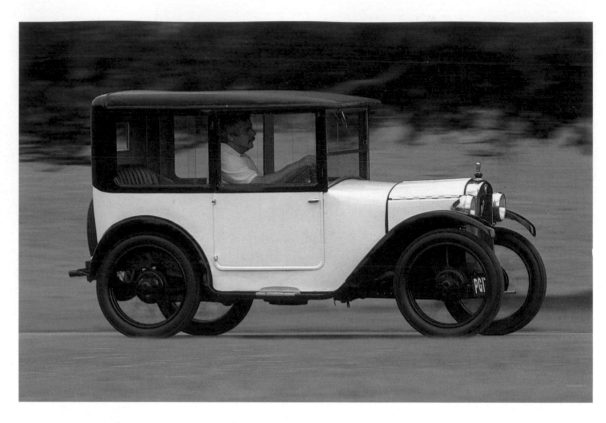

The bare and typically vintage dashboard of a 1928 Austin Seven 'Chummy.'

The Seven engine was a simple but beautifully executed flathead four, initially of 696cc but more generally of 747cc.

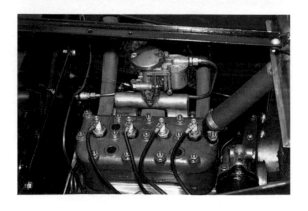

The original factory Austin Seven saloon was known as the 'Top Hat' model, for obvious reasons! This is a 1928-9 car.

choice: the first of the MG Midgets.

It is difficult to overstate the significance of this modest little fabric-bodied sports car. Based on the chassis and mechanicals of the humble overhead-cam Morris Minor, the M type Midget established the MG as a marque and through the models it spawned placed the firm at the forefront of the international sporting scene.

Whether in four-cylinder Midget form or as a larger six-cylinder, the MG excelled in every branch of the sport. The Midget itself established the essential MG character of a good-natured and fast but not over-fast sports car at a reasonable price. And who would dare sneer at an engine that started out delivering 20bhp in the M type and ended up pushing out 146bhp in its ultimate supercharged development, for record breaking in Germany?

The MG was the product of a small team of engineers who resourcefully adapted essentially prosaic mechanicals to achieve results out of all proportion to the money spent. In complete contrast to this down-to-earth approach was that of another of the great names: Bugatti.

Bugatti: artistry in metal

Ettore Bugatti was an artist as much as an engineer, and his cars had a sculptural elegance in their engineering that made British counterparts such as the Bentley seem positively agricultural. Added to this was the inspired grace of the coachwork, often to the

France's answer to the Austin Seven was the cruder but undoubtedly charming Citroën 5CV. To the forefront of the photo is a 5CV with *camionnette normande* bodywork: there is a drop-down tailgate and the passenger seat back folds to one side to allow long loads to be carried. Behind is an example of the upmarket cabriolet, and to the rear is the basic *torpédo* model.

The supercharged Bentley 4½-liter stripped bare. Most immediately noticeable feature is the supercharger hung between the front dumb-irons. Fuelled by two SU carbs, it pushed power to 182bhp.

designs of Bugatti's talented son Jean. Yet the Bugatti was no ultimately empty demonstration of style over substance. On the contrary: the aesthetic precision was matched to a spine-tingling mechanical effectiveness that made the Bugatti one of the most desirable marques of the time. Even today that cachet is undiminished.

During the vintage period Bugatti's fame mainly derived from his Type 35 Grand Prix model, which won over 1500 races during its career, and is one of the world's most successful GP cars of all time. This slender pointed-tail racer with its narrow horseshoe radiator had a delightful free-revving straight-eight engine with roller-bearing crankshaft. Among its distinctive features were cast alloy wheels with integral brake drums, a hollow tube front axle through which the springs passed, and a body braced by criss-crossed piano wire. Taut, predictable and balanced, its behaviour on the track mirrored the elegance of its engineering.

The most famous Bullnose of all: the 1925 Morris Garages special known as 'Old Number One' and erroneously regarded as the first MG. It had an overhead-valve version of the normal 11.9hp Hotchkiss engine, and was built for MG founder Cecil Kimber. He had begun building special-bodied Morris Garages Bullnoses in 1923.

This 3-liter Bentley is a replica of the 1927 Le Mans winner, and was built from scratch around a wrecked chassis.

History has tended to distort our view of the roadgoing Bugattis: in the vintage era these were often rather more ordinary than the marque's reputation might lead us to expect. The four-cylinder Type 40 for instance, was referred to as Bugatti's Morris Cowley; and the first of the touring straight-eights, the Type 30 of 1922, has been stigmatized by two leading writers as 'a fairly bad car' — rough, noisy, and not very fast. However, against such models must be set the splendid supercharged Type 43, effectively a roadgoing Type 35B, and the competent and balanced — if less overtly sporting — Type 44.

The legendary Royale of 1927 is a different matter entirely. Only six were built, and this massive 12.8-liter extravagance must surely be classed as the supreme motoring white elephant. Yet the translation of Ettore Bugatti's engineering flair on to such a large scale produced a car that was far less of a juggernaut to drive than its wheelbase of over 14ft (4.27m) would suggest.

More relevant in motoring terms was the 'mini-Royale' Type 46 of 1929, an impressive luxury model that became even more of a delight when its 5.3-liter engine was supercharged. It was to be the 1930s, however, before Bugatti's prestige reached its zenith. The best was yet to come.

Alfa Romeo and Lancia

The fortunes of Alfa Romeo followed a similar course: competition-based glory in the 1920s opening out into touring car glamour in the 1930s — although in Alfa's case the competition successes continued throughout the latter decade.

The Milan manufacturer began operations in 1909, and after the First World War soon distinguished itself in sporting events. Its rise to prominence began in earnest in 1924, when former Fiat engineer Vittorio Jano designed the straight-eight double-overhead-cam P2 racing car. With this Alfa Romeo won the very first *grande épreuve* it entered, the 1924 French GP. The following year the company was declared World Champion.

From the P2 Jano developed the single-ohc 1½-liter Type 6C six-cylinder of 1927, which soon became available in double-ohc form, optionally supercharged. A 1750cc dohc version followed, and this was notably successful in most sporting events. With its smooth and potent engine, and excellent chassis, the 1750 was one of Europe's great vintage and post-vintage sports cars, and established an Alfa Romeo character that has survived to this day.

Fellow Italian marque Lancia began building a rather different image during the vintage years: that of creative, free-

A genuine Le Mans car: this is the Speed Six Bentley that came second in the 1930 race. The Speed Six was a short-wheelbase tuned version of the six-cylinder 6½-liter that had been introduced in 1925 to cater for those wanting a Bentley chassis more suited to carrying heavy closed coachwork.

thinking engineering, idiosyncratic perhaps, but always logical and generally in advance of that of its competitors.

The Lambda of 1922 showed the way — and proved beyond contest the engineering talents of Vincenzo Lancia. The principal feature of the 2120cc Lambda was its combined chassis and body frame, a predecessor of the modern monocoque that gave a rigid and light structure. For 1922 this was truly revolutionary, and was married to independent sliding-pillar front suspension and a narrow-angle V4 engine with overhead camshaft. Weight of the open tourer was only 1870lb (848kg), handling was superb, and the model lasted until 1931.

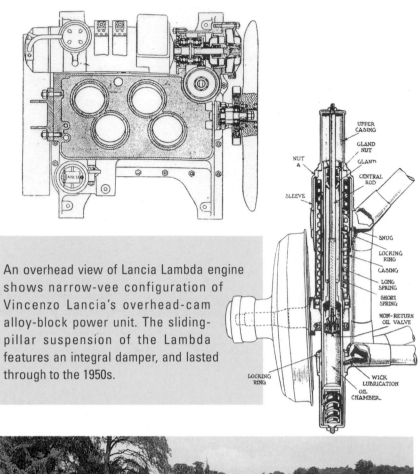

An overhead view of Lancia Lambda engine shows narrow-vee configuration of Vincenzo Lancia's overhead-cam alloy-block power unit. The sliding-pillar suspension of the Lambda features an integral damper, and lasted through to the 1950s.

Last of the Edwardians: the Vauxhall 30/98. The yellow car is a boat-tailed Wensum model (with no doors to the body); the other two cars are examples of the regular Velox four-seater tourer.

Hair-shirt British sports car motoring at its best: the chain-driven Frazer Nash. This is a 1926 Speed model. The Frazer Nash chain transmission allows quick changes without double declutching, and the cars have delightful handling.

Aesthetic perfection! Could any racing car be more gorgeous than the Type 35 Bugatti? This is a Type 35B, which means that it has a supercharger to boost power of the straight-eight overhead-cam engine.

Rolling thunder: the vintage Mercedes

The two premier Italian sporting marques provided subtle pleasures. From Germany came automotive gratification of a rather more demonstrative kind, provided by Mercedes, which from 1926 was allied to the Benz company.

Mercedes pioneered supercharging for production cars in 1921, and by 1923 its flagship model was a blown 6-liter. From this was developed a short-wheelbase variant, the Model K. The blower was worked via a multi-plate clutch, and only engaged when the accelerator was fully depressed. In normal use the car was not notably fast, and it was a handful to drive. From this inauspicious beginning sprang four of the most famous cars to carry the three-pointed star.

In 1927 the Model S had its debut. The six-cylinder engine of the Model K was enlarged to 6.8 liters, and there was a new chassis, underslung at the rear and with the engine set further back in the frame. Although still a muscle-developing monster to handle, it was less of a battle to drive fast than its predecessor. In 1928 it chalked up over 50 victories, and gave birth to a 7-liter version, the SS. With the blower engaged this developed a heady 200bhp.

Motor racing successes continued and prompted Mercedes-Benz into building 31 short-wheelbase SSK models, primarily for German hill-climb events. With a raised compression ratio, 220bhp was attainable, or a fearsome 300bhp with a special large-displacement supercharger.

The final evolution of the series was the lightweight SSKL of 1931, which was extensively drilled for lightness. Only seven were built, and one was taken to an epic victory in 1931 in the Italian Mille Miglia event.

Nobody could accuse these 'blood and thunder' Mercedes of having finesse. Even their most enthusiastic devotees concede they are something of a beast to drive, while the less charitable see them as being all noise and aggression, with less usable performance than far humbler vehicles. Never in doubt, however, is a forceful charisma and sheer presence that is unmistakably German.

Luxury without compromise

Moving to the carriage trade end of the market, to luxury tourers rather than sports cars, we enter the realms of some of the very greatest motor cars of any time.

Foremost among these is the French-built Hispano-Suiza, created by the esteemed Swiss engineer Marc Birkigt. When the 6.6-liter H6 model came out in 1919 it was a sensation, so far in advance was it of any competition. Its alloy-block overhead-cam six was half a planned V12 aero engine, and featured a seven-bearing crankshaft machined from the solid and twin-coil ignition with two plugs per cylinder. Installed in a deep and stiff chassis, this gorgeous engine pushed out 135bhp and delivered effortless mid-range power.

Light and easy to control, with an undemanding gear change and sharp steering, the Hispano set standards with its speed, good handling and comfort: not to mention its superb and ingenious servo-assisted four-wheel brakes, which were subsequently adopted

by Rolls-Royce. An 8-liter version followed, and was good for 100mph (160km/h), as against the 75–85mph (120–137km/h) of the 6.6-liter. In addition a short-wheelbase chassis was offered for sporting coachwork, and such cars performed most capably.

Vying for the same market was Italy's finest, the Isotta-Fraschini. The Isotta's excellence has never been doubted, but in engineering terms it has invariably been less highly regarded than the standard-setting Hispano. Even so, the alloy-block pushrod straight-eight Tipo 8 of 1919 was unquestionably a superb car. It became even more so with the 1925 introduction of the Tipo 8A, with an enlarged engine of 7.4 liters. Sticking to a one-model policy, Isotta developed into one of the most glamorous of marques. This was in no small part due to the stylish coachwork by top Italian houses Castagna and Sala that its chassis so often carried: 'exercises in self-propelled architecture', said one writer.

The Isotta was also well received in the United States, where Fleetwood and LeBaron bodied many cars, and where total sales of 450 were racked up in the 1919-32 period. Such dependence on the US market hastened Isotta's demise, however, and its sales collapsed as the Great Depression took hold. Only 30 of an improved but expensive and unsaleable Tipo 8B were made before production petered out at the beginning of the 1930s.

The extraordinary Bugatti Type 41, better known as the Royale. Only six were built, as the intended royal customers did not materialize. This left Bugatti with a stock of Royale engines, so he diversified into railcar manufacture, and in total 79 railcars with adapted Royale power units were built. This particular Royale carries two-door coachwork by Kellner of Paris and was exhibited at the 1932 London motor show.

Simple interior of Kellner-bodied Bugatti Royale — no speedometer or fuel gauge.

America's finest

In any case, America had its own top-notch manufacturers in particular Duesenberg, Packard, and latterly the upstart Cord.

Duesenberg's fame is due essentially to one car: the 1928 Model J and its derivatives. In 1926 flamboyant super-salesman Errett Lobban Cord had bought the Duesenberg firm, already well-known for the advanced engineering of its overhead-cam straight-eight Model A. He wanted his new acquisition to offer the finest car in America, and with the Model J he is generally held to have succeeded in this aim. Certainly the 6.9-liter straight-eight Model J was ahead of the competition on engine specification alone: no other US manufacturer offered a double-ohc four valve per cylinder power unit at the time.

But this was not all: the Model J carried some of the most striking bodywork of any car, designed by the inspired Gordon Buehrig and built by America's top coachbuilders. With its conventional but well-executed chassis, the Model J was fast, refined and well-mannered, despite its bulk. There was more to come, with a supercharged version, the SJ, launched in 1932. This was claimed — questionably — to deliver 320bhp.

Italian great: the Alfa Romeo 6C-1750. This fabric-bodied example has the supercharged engine and dates from 1930. Its owner Adrian Lydell is at the wheel.

The vintage Packard was 'old money' in contrast to the 'new money' of the glitzy but accomplished Duesenberg. Well-engineered but unobtrusively styled, the Packard dominated the upper reaches of the market in the later 1920s. The company established its prestige reputation with the Twin Six of 1915. In 1923 this was replaced by a straight-eight, again a flathead, and this decent-handling and well-made model was a favourite among the discriminating rich. Packard had the good sense not to rely on the eight, however, and a humbler six-cylinder car was in fact the firm's best seller in this period.

Quite what the average Packard buyer thought of the 1929 Cord L-29 is something to ponder. E.L.Cord took no half-measures when he decided to launch a car carrying his own name, and the L-29 boasted front-wheel drive and, as a result, sensationally low-slung bodywork. But maintenance was problematic, and the year of the Wall Street crash was hardly the best time to launch a flashy, extravagantly priced car. Production ceased in 1932 after only 4400 L-29s had been sold.

Lancia's Lambda of 1922-31 was a technical landmark, with its lightweight unitary body frame and chassis, V4 engine, and sliding-pillar independent front suspension. The radiator surround was a stressed member, carrying the mounting stays for the front suspension.

This SSK is almost the ultimate of the vintage era supercharged Mercedes models: only the seven-off ultra-lightweight SSKL comes above it in desirability. The SSK was intended as a hill-climb special, and had a short chassis and a power output of 220bhp with the supercharger engaged.

The Model S was the first of the series and introduced the new underslung sports chassis. The new model scored a 1-2-3 victory for Mercedes in the 1927 German GP and production began in 1928. A total of 149 were built.

Rolls-Royce: a recipe for survival

Unfortunately, Cord and Duesenberg were not to last out the 1930s. In contrast, one manufacturer remained at the forefront of the worldwide luxury car business throughout the pre-Second World War era, following a conservative but never narrow-minded model policy that would ensure its long-term survival. That company was Rolls-Royce.

In 1925 came a replacement for the 40/50 Silver Ghost — the New Phantom, or Phantom I, as it was to be called retrospectively. This was essentially a revised engine with overhead valves in the old 40/50 chassis. The result was enhanced performance with no loss of the legendary Rolls-Royce refinement.

This considered evolution of an Edwardian design was displaced in 1929 by the altogether more contemporary Phantom II. The engine was now of monobloc construction, and around 20 per cent more powerful, the gearbox was four-speed and in unit with it, and there was a new chassis that dispensed with the antiquated cantilever rear springs.

Despite the bodies it carried which tended to result in fairly

One of the pinnacles of vintage engineering was the Hispano-Suiza H6. This evolved into the bigger-engined 8-liter H6B, of which this is a 1929 model with coachwork by Kellner of Paris.

weighty cars, the Phantom II was good for over 80mph (129kph) — although at first refinement was surprisingly disappointing. For those who found the new car a little too heavy and ponderous, in 1931 the Phantom II Continental was announced, built on the short-wheelbase chassis and with a more powerful engine and stiffer springing. Attracting the very finest of British coachwork, especially on the Continental, the Phantom II held a more assured position among luxury cars than any other.

That was all very well, but dependence on a single ultra-high-cost model was no ticket to survival. Rolls-Royce was not too proud to admit this, and in 1922 the firm launched a small 20hp car, with a 3.1-liter overhead-valve six. Progressively developed, it became the mainstay of the Rolls-Royce range, substantially outselling the Phantoms and still retaining all the prestige of the Rolls-Royce marque.

Such level-headedness was to serve the company well in the exciting but unstable 1930s, when the great cars became ever more extravagant but also when so many concerns were to go to the wall. As the vintage era ended, however, styling and technology were posed for a heady decade of intoxicating progress.

GREAT CARS OF THE WORLD

Few Isotta-Fraschini 8As come more flamboyant than this white-tyred roadster of 1926, built by the American firm Fleetwood to a design by LeBaron: but then it was ordered by heart-throb Rudolph Valentino who, alas, died before he could take delivery. Power comes from a 7.4-liter overhead-valve straight-eight.

America's top car, the Duesenberg Model J. It was introduced in 1928 and was later joined by a supercharged SJ variant. The engine is a twin-cam straight-eight with four valves per cylinder — an unusually advanced choice of power unit for an American car of the period.

The Cord L-29 of 1929 introduced front-wheel drive to the American market. Service problems meant that the car did not live up to the promise of its low-slung good looks, and few were sold.

The Phantom II in more sporting Continental form: in this case a 1931 model with a slightly later body by the Carlton Carriage Company. Coachwork on the Phantom II was not normally this sporty.

The Rolls-Royce Phantom I used an overhead valve version of the 40/50 Silver Ghost engine, and retained the earlier car's chassis. This 1927 example carries sedanca de ville bodywork by Hooper and was built for the manager of the Plaza Hotel in New York.

More representative of the type is this 1934 Phantom II — although the body is actually a modern re-creation of the Windover original, because the car was at some stage converted into a hearse.

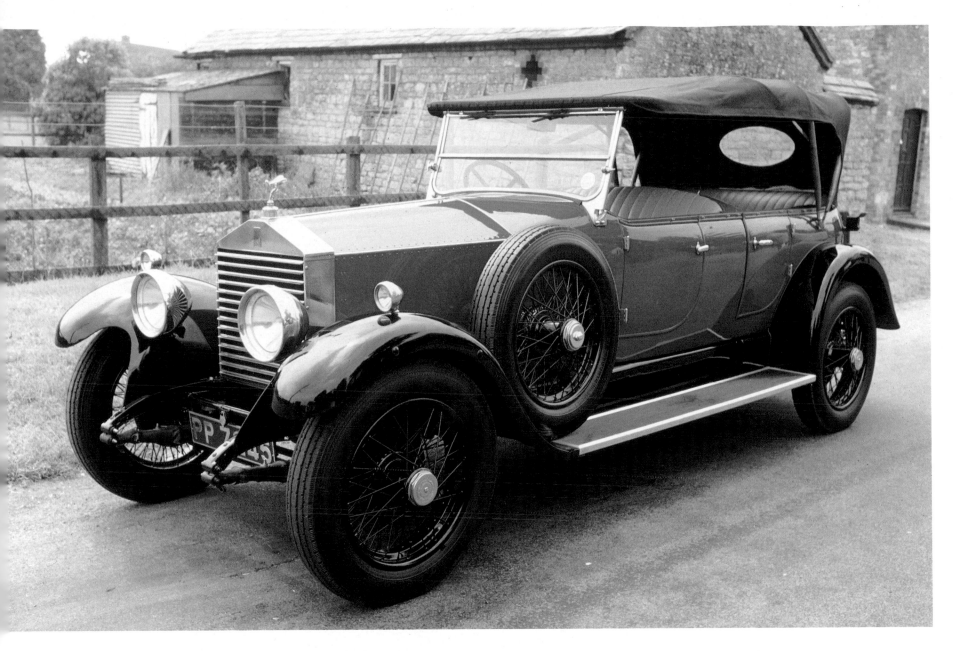

The 'baby' Rolls-Royce in its original form: a 20hp model from 1926. In common with many such cars, this example has been rebodied as a barrel-sided open tourer, a cheaper and more remunerative process than giving it a reproduction of the closed or drophead coachwork the car probably carried in the first place.

The Cadillac V16 was the world's first production car with such an engine. This example dates from 1931 and carries sports phaeton bodywork. It was originally owned by an Indian maharajah, who used it for tiger hunting.

3

Prewar Magnificence

The love affair with extravagant engineering and high style continued without hesitation into the 1930s. This was despite a worldwide recession that ultimately eliminated many manufacturers — especially those unable or unwilling to meet the demands of a changing and more developed market.

The more cylinders the better?

On the mechanical side, engines did not just have to be big — they had to be multi-cylindered. Cadillac led the way, with its V16, announced at the end of 1929.

The world's first V16 production car, its overhead-valve 7.4-liter engine developed only 165bhp, but effortlessly smooth performance was matched to unparalleled pulling power, thanks to a stupendous 300lbft (407Nm) of torque.

But following the Wall Street crash, who wanted such indulgent transportation? Not very many: after sales of over 3000 in the V16's first year, annual registrations dropped swiftly to around 50 cars a year. In 1937 a new V16 was introduced, with a lighter and simpler flathead engine. This was more successful, selling over 500 examples in three seasons. Without their V12s and V8s of the 1930s, however, Cadillac would have been scuppered.

Another American firm, the Indianapolis-based Marmon, was also brave enough to try a V16, and its advanced alloy 8.1-liter of 1931 developed an impressive 200bhp. Despite its respected straight-eights, however, the small company lacked the financial strength to sustain such an extravagance, and car manufacture ceased in 1933.

Below the V16s came a raft of V12 luxury cars: during the 1930s this became the accepted top-of-the-range configuration for prestige manufacturers in most countries. In the United States,

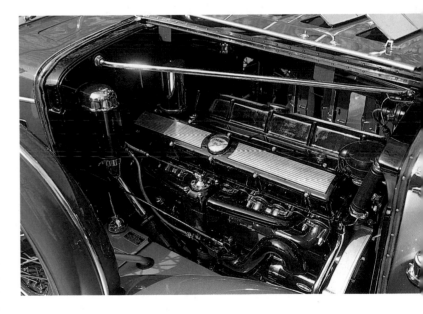

Cadillac offered a V12 that was in effect three-quarters of its V16, and in the 1931–7 period sold 10,821 of this 6-liter model. But the successful evolution of the Cadillac V8 led to its developing as much power as the twelve, so in 1937 the bigger car was deleted — a logical move, as the new V16 was cheaper to produce, and lighter.

Lincoln fished in the same pool. A Ford subsidiary since 1922, it was managed by Henry Ford's son Edsel (1893–1943), who in 1932 put into production a V12 of 7.2 liters. A 6.2-liter joined the range a year later, but soon both were replaced by a single 6.8-liter model with an engine that drew on Ford V8 practice and was cheaper to produce. Fine cars, these restrained K series Lincolns were nonetheless a minority interest. Edsel Ford accordingly pushed ahead with a 'poor man's Lincoln', drawing on the Ford parts bin — the Zephyr.

Announced for 1936, the Zephyr was not one of the greats, but with its unitary construction, V12 engine and streamlined Art Deco styling it was undeniably an appealing package. From it was developed the upmarket 1940–8 Lincoln Continental.

Of altogether more assured status was Packard's V12. Introduced for 1932, it marked a return by the top mainstream US manufacturer to the configuration it had pioneered back in 1915. The 7.3-liter Twelve sold 13,400 up until its deletion in 1939 — pretty good going. Later models had a 7.7-liter engine, and independent front suspension and hydraulic brakes came in for 1937. An unusual feature of the engine was inclined side valves actuated by roller-bearing hydraulic lifters.

Packard engineering was essentially conservative, but the detailing and execution were first rate; in the case of the Twelve this gave superb refinement and an impressive turn of speed, together with good road manners. Unfortunately, the V12 was an expensive to make distraction from the various lesser Packard straight-eights.

Indeed, the top of range eights — magnificent cars in their own right — were themselves not financially viable. As the 1930s progressed, therefore, the various models began to share more components, while the best seller was a modest six-cylinder model. The magic of the upper-crust Packard was slipping away.

Over in Europe the V12 was also in fashion, led by Hispano-Suiza, whose extravagant Type 68 of 1931–8 offered 250bhp in its ultimate 11.3-liter form. With a chassis costing £1000 more than that of a Rolls-Royce Phantom II (chassis price £1750 for 1932) there were few takers, despite the Hispano's acknowledged excellence of engineering.

In Germany both Horch and Maybach came up with V12s. Horch's example was short-lived, and during the 1930s the company majored on stolid and well-engineered straight-eights and a lower-priced range of V8s. Maybach, meanwhile, persisted until 1939 with its V12, first seen ten years earlier. In 8-liter Zeppelin

Lagonda V12 chassis is a typically substantial affair, with hefty cruciform and deep side sections. The independent front suspension uses short torsion bars — rather shorter than is best for supple springing. The 4½-liter engine was designed by a team led by W. O. Bentley.

form this was a fearsome beast, weighing up to 6720lb (3048kg) or 3½ tons. It had the legendary *Doppelschnellgang* or double-shift gearbox, which meant there were eight forward gears and four reverse. Smaller six-cylinder Maybachs of the period were more manageable, almost as imposing in a characteristically German way, and certainly they rate as some of the Reich's finest cars.

Finally, Great Britain fielded two of the very best of the V12 breed: the Rolls-Royce Phantom III and the Lagonda V12. The former was introduced in 1935, its 7340cc V12 installed in a new chassis with independent front suspension. With the civilized behaviour and mechanical smoothness expected of a Rolls-Royce, the new car immediately put Britain at the top of the tree as far as luxury cars were concerned.

The Lagonda V12 of 1937 had the Rolls-Royce in its sights, and its designer, W. O. Bentley, was doubtless keen to best the firm that had bought Bentley Motors from the receiver six years before. But 'W. O.' evidently found it hard to design a car without putting sporting characteristics above touring refinement: notwithstanding his requirement for the Lagonda that it should be capable of accelerating from rest to maximum speed in top gear.

Fast the 4½-liter V12 certainly was, with its free-revving unusually short-stroke engine, but for a Rolls rival refinement was lacking, and the car was regarded as something of a brute to drive. The promise was there, however, and it has to be regretted that the Second World War cut short further development of the model.

Lincoln offered an upmarket V12 during the 1930s. The 6.8-liter flathead engine in this 1938 model draws on Ford V8 practice and the coupé bodywork is by LeBaron.

Brutality versus finesse

There were no fancy V12s from Mercedes other than a run of 23 such cars made for top Nazis during the period 1938–42. Instead the Stuttgart firm concentrated on a series of supercharged straight-eights, with the mammoth 7.6-liter Grosser Mercedes for heads of state and others who found lesser vehicles too common.

Starting with the 380K of 1933, the blown Mercedes progressed through 500K, 540K and 580K versions; maximum power, with supercharger engaged, climbed from 120bhp in the 380K to 180bhp in the 580K. Noteworthy features were a modern twin-wishbone front suspension and a swing-axle rear, together with servo-assisted hydraulic brakes. Assertive cabriolet bodywork was common, some of the styles having a brutal grace that still takes the breath away.

In Italy an altogether more elegant approach to engineering was shown by Alfa Romeo, whose 8C–2300 of 1931–4 was one of the ultimate sports cars of its day. Its supercharged twin-cam straight-eight was a detuned racing unit, and the car was as at home in competition as on the open road.

The 8C–2300 was in effect succeeded by the 8C–2900, a car that has inspired more rhapsodic enthusiasm than virtually any other prewar vehicle. Originally devised to use up stocks of leftover

racing engines, the twin-supercharged 2900 was the supreme melding of Alfa's road and race technologies, combining an exquisitely engineered all-independent chassis with some of the most stunning of coachbuilder Touring's streamlined bodies. As a potent yet delightfully refined road car it was without parallel, and as a competition machine it won three Mille Miglias in a row and gave a dominant performance at the 1938 Le Mans.

By the end of the 1930s Bugatti, in contrast, had lost its competitive edge, as it failed to keep abreast of engineering advances. Yet that did not stop the company producing some of the most stunning road cars of the decade. Into the Type 43's shoes stepped another magnificent sports car derived from a Bugatti Grand Prix model. Whereas the Type 43 used the engine of the Type 35B racer, the new 110mph (177km/h) Type 55 had the twin-cam power unit of the Type 51 GP car. It had something rather more, though: the glorious sweeping lines of the roadster body styled by Jean Bugatti. Not without reason is it today one of the most valuable of the road going Bugattis.

On the touring car side, the 'mini-Royale' Type 46 evolved into the supercharged twin-cam Type 50, and the more modest Type 44 was replaced in 1930 by the 3.3-liter single-cam Type 49. Regarded as 'the finest of all touring Bugattis' by one critic, the sweet-natured Type 49 gave way in 1934 to one of the most legendary of Bugattis: the Type 57.

With this twin-cam 3.3-liter, Bugatti embarked on what was practically a single-model policy, and the Type 57 in its various forms become the mainstay of his range up until the Second World War. Available with or without supercharger, the Type 57 carried some of the most breathtakingly rakish of coachwork, frequently by Jean Bugatti.

These designs were at their most captivating when on the lowered and shortened 'S' chassis, which featured an aggressively V-shaped radiator as an outer sign of the uprated dry-sump engine under the bonnet. Most extraordinary of all was the Atlantic coupé, with its riveted aluminium body — complete with dorsal spine running from windscreen to rear bumper.

Under the elegant skin, however, the Bugatti was stagnating: independent front suspension was tried and then discarded, hydraulic brakes only came in 1938, and Ettore Bugatti seemed to be losing interest in car making. After Jean Bugatti was killed in a road accident in 1939 the future of the firm began to look grim indeed.

Lincoln's unitary construction Zephyr was a distinctly more affordable V12, and was very much Ford-derived in its mechanicals: down to the traditional Ford transverse-leaf springing. In its final form the flathead V12 was of 4817cc capacity.

French renaissance

Rather more encouraging was the renaissance of the French specialist firms Delahaye, Delage and Talbot. All had begun the 1930s with products of limited distinction, but were to end it with high-prestige ranges of fine cars.

Delahaye's 1930s success was based on the sensible evolution of sound but unspectacular engineering. The company's 18CV model of 1933 shared its conventional although lightweight ohv six with trucks and fire engines, but proved its potential when a short-wheelbase Sport version acquited itself well in the Alpine Trial. This led to a competition model, a 5th place at the 1935 Le Mans, and thence to the introduction of the Type 135, a 3½-liter good for 110mph (177km/h), or rather more in 155bhp form.

A refined grand tourer of refreshing modernity, with an excellent ride, the Type 135 carried some of France's finest coachwork. The remark of one historian that in comparison with the Bugatti it was more 'uprated hack than downrated racehorse' should not be taken as any slur on the abilities of the car — least of all in its demonstrably effective sports car form, in which it scored many successes.

Delage entered the 1930s with the D8 straight-eight, a substantial and smooth-running 4-liter touring model that attracted some splendid formal coachwork. In 1935 Delahaye took over the firm, and the final prewar Delage, the D8-120, featured a Delahaye-based engine and a Delahaye design of chassis. More to the point, as with preceding models, the new car was often bodied with some of the most outrageous of creations from French coachbuilders such as Figoni et Falaschi and Saoutchik.

Talbot's rebirth came when Antony Lago disentangled the firm from the wreckage of the failed Anglo-French Sunbeam-Talbot-Darracq combine in 1934. Lago's recipe for the marque was to give it a sporting image through participation in competition, and to establish a clear technical link between the touring models and their competition counterparts.

Starting point for this process was the Type 150 of 1934. For this new model Lago took the existing straight-six and gave it a high-performance hemispherical alloy head — while retaining pushrod actuation for the valves. This arrangement was later used by BMW, and later still by Chrysler for its famed 'hemi'.

With its underslung chassis and well-proportioned factory coachwork, the T150 looked assured of success. There was, however, a slight hiccup in Lago's competition plans: a change in racing regulations put the T150's 2996cc engine uneasily in the middle of a new 2-liter to 4-liter class. Accordingly the power unit was enlarged to 3996cc.

The resultant T150C was just what was needed. In competition it soon proved its mettle, while as the Lago Special road car it seemed a perfect expression of the GT ideal, combining a race-bred chassis with elegant luxury coachwork. This was sometimes flamboyantly bodied in tear drop aerodynamic coupé form by the French company Figoni et Falaschi.

The Lago Special cost much the same as a Bugatti Type 57. For the bulk of his sales Lago therefore relied on a simplified 3-liter with conventional valve gear. There was also an orthodox ohv 4-liter, and both series were generally seen with refined and understated factory coachwork. Without a doubt these were the golden years of the Talbot marque.

American flamboyance

Such European delights were a world apart from the less subtle American interpretations of the specialist-manufactured 'personal' car. This was a dying breed by the mid-1930s, but that did not stop E. L. Cord from putting into production two of the most striking examples, the Auburn Speedster and the Cord 810/812.

Despite the failure of its V12, the glamour days were not over for beleaguered Auburn. Based on an obsolete bodyshell of which large stocks remained, the Speedster of 1935–7 was an inspired scissors-and-paste job that resulted in one of the most dramatically styled American cars of the late 1930s. When supercharged, the straight-eight Speedster had the performance to match its looks, as well as the added enhancement of chromed external exhaust pipes. This was a lazy performance, though, with none of the crispness of more thoroughbred machinery, while the behaviour of the softly suspended chassis was similarly unsporting.

In spite of its competitive price and its good looks, shared by a four-door phaeton model, Auburn sales still continued to plummet: high style alone clearly was not sufficient to save the Cord empire. Nor, alas, was high style and high technology, as the stunning Cord so sadly proved.

Dramatic and daring, the Cord 810 of 1935 and its supercharged 812 sibling were the most modern cars the United States produced until the 1960s: yet they were made on a wing and a prayer by a small company on its last legs.

The body was Gordon Buehrig's masterpiece, with concealed wind-up headlamps, no running boards or conventional radiator shell, concealed door hinges, and a fully disappearing top on the convertible: no car of the era even approached it for such imposing cleanness of line. And underneath this rolling art form there was technology to match: front-wheel drive, roller-bearing trailing-arm independent front suspension, electro-vacuum gearshift, and a chassis-less monocoque structure. The Lycoming flathead V8 engine was no technical wonder, but when supercharged (for 1937) it delivered a more than adequate 170bhp.

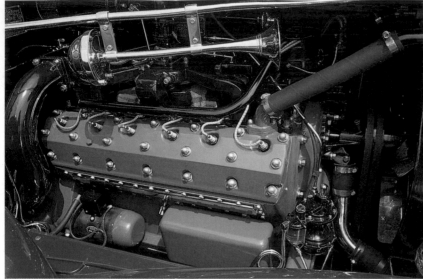

Packard's second generation V12 was introduced for 1932. This is a 1934 Dietrich-bodied Victoria convertible. The engine used steeply inclined side valves operated by roller-bearing rockers; the tappets were hydraulically operated, as indeed were those on the Cadillac V16, and the cylinder heads were in aluminium.

Yet the car was improvisation at its finest. The headlamp mechanisms were adapted from aircraft landing light assemblies; the instruments and the interior handles were bought-out job lots; there were only two dies used for the doors of the four-door saloon, the roof of which was welded up from several pieces, because Cord did not have a large enough press...

Although reliability was never wonderful, the Cord worked: it offered purring power, a smooth but not floaty ride, light and responsive steering, and decent cornering ability. It also cost twice as much as a Cadillac. Within two years the Cord was dead, and with it the Auburn-Cord-Duesenberg empire.

Thoroughbreds and giant-killers

Compared to high-class British cars of the time, the aberrant Cord must have seemed as if it came from another planet but although conservative, top-ranking British cars of the period were nonetheless some of the world's finest.

Foremost among them was the reborn Bentley, now dubbed The Silent Sports Car by its makers Rolls-Royce. That was a fair description: the 3½-liter and subsequent 4¼-liter Bentleys had impressive performance and a taut chassis, but at the same time were refined and smooth-riding in a manner alien to their glorious predecessors.

Built on a chassis intended for a discarded small Rolls-Royce, and with an uprated Rolls-Royce 20/25 engine, these 'Derby' Bentleys were fine vehicles in their own right. Smaller and lighter than their Rolls-Royce cousins, they attracted some of the finest sporting coachwork of the later 1930s.

Meanwhile, Bentley's perceived role as a purveyor of no-

nonsense high-performance sports cars had passed in some extent to Invicta, who from 1925 had been offering a straightforward sporting six powered by a proprietary Meadows engine.

This car was something of a challenge to drive fast, but Donald Healey took one to victory in the 1931 Monte Carlo Rally, and to 2nd place in the 1932 event, despite his reservations about its roadholding and handling. Its ultimate replacement, the Hudson-engined Railton, was possibly a better car, despite the jibes about it being an 'Anglo-American bastard'.

Then there was the Lagonda, a marque that gained significantly in stature during the 1930s — especially after W. O. Bentley joined the company in 1935, as chief designer. The 4½-liter model introduced for 1934 was promising material, and a 4th place in the 1934 Tourist Trophy led to the creation of the beefed-up short-wheelbase M45R Rapide which won the 1935 Le Mans race.

'W. O.' considerably civilized the Lagonda, and this process culminated in the magnificent LG45 Rapide introduced in 1936. Torquey and docile, the Rapide was a captivating amalgam of British and American styling, built around finely honed traditional British mechanicals.

If such fine machines were beyond your pocket, other respected cars were available at lesser prices, such as the Talbot of Swiss designer Georges Roesch or perhaps the surprisingly advanced big Alvis. Fast, sporting and well-mannered, the Alvis Speed 20 and subsequent Speed 25 and 4.3-liter models boasted both independent front suspension and an all-synchromesh gearbox. The Talbot was rather more 'old school', but its high-efficiency ohv engines and well-executed chassis resulted in a delightful-to-drive sporting car that chalked up many competition successes.

Besides these upper-crust British marques there was still plenty of choice in sporting machinery from manufacturers such as Riley, Triumph and SS Cars. Indeed, SS came up with what is today one of the most sought-after of late 1930s sports cars: the SS Jaguar 100. With its flowing lines it was almost too rakishly attractive for its own good, especially as its mechanicals were fairly prosaic and its price so modest. It was regarded as a cheapskate 'Promenade Percy' sports car by those who could afford to pay half as much again for a BMW 328, but that was something of a slight on a machine that performed strongly and was generally agreeable to drive.

The BMW was of course something special, and is generally

Packard's money earners were the lesser six-cylinder and eight-cylinder models. This is a 1937 Super Eight, with limousine bodywork on a 139in (3.5m) wheelbase.

Hispano-Suiza also offered a V12, and this splendid example carries
coachwork by Saoutchik. Only 76 of the V12 were made.

regarded as the finest sporting all-rounder of the pre-Second World
War years, successful in everything from circuit racing to rallying
and trials. This connoisseur's sports car with its semi-streamlined
body had a well-engineered chassis with independent front
suspension and hydraulic brakes, and featured a hemi-head 2-liter
six-cylinder with ingenious pushrod-actuated valves. It was far in
advance of any other series production sports model, and set a
benchmark for other manufacturers.

Rather more traditional — primitive, even — was the British
MG, which reached its prewar sporting pinnacle with the Magnette
K3. This supercharged 1087cc giant-killer developed a lusty 120bhp
and was successful enough in competition to be adopted by the

great Italian driver Tazio Nuvolari, who took a K3 to victory in the
1933 Tourist Trophy.

Cecil Kimber, the head of MG, ensured that the small British
firm had a high profile in all forms of motor sport, and developed
models such as the K3 specifically for racing. This progress
culminated in the ultra-advanced R-type single-seater of 1935, with
its backbone chassis and all-round independent torsion-bar
suspension. Alas, MG's participation in competition was seen as an
expensive diversion, and in addition the ordinary touring MGs were
relatively costly to produce, so in 1935 the company was brought
under the direct control of Morris Motors.

Typically German in style, this straight-eight Horch model 853A sports cabriolet is a 1938 model. By this stage the front suspension was independent and the rear used a De Dion axle.

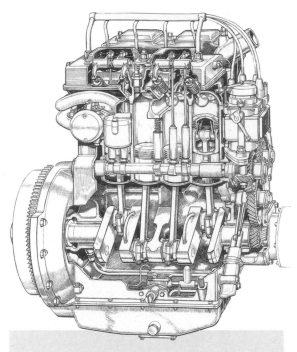

Riley's long-lived twin-cam engine was first seen in 1926 and derivatives were still current as late as 1957. In this cutaway of an early engine the layout of the high-set camshafts and short pushrods is clearly visible. The inclined valves allow hemispherical combustion chambers.

Technology and the popular car

The most significant achievements of the 1930s were not, however, in the domain of sports cars or cost-no-object luxury cars. Rather, the most crucial development was the way technology caught up with the popular car. This was less the case in Britain and in the United States, both of which were tardy in adopting the advances of the decade: primarily it was continental Europe that had the courage to push engineering boundaries forward.

Few were more courageous than that inspired gambler André Citroën, who initiated one of the greatest engineering achievements of all time, the Traction Avant (or front-wheel-drive) Citroën of 1934. Although none of its features were in themselves new, to combine in a single car front-wheel drive, torsion-bar independent suspension, monocoque construction and a wet-liner overhead-valve engine with 'floating power' mounting — not to mention hydraulic brakes and, from 1936, rack and pinion steering — was indeed a technical *tour de force*. Not only that, but a long, low, feline stance and a complete harmony of line make the Citroën supremely good-looking. Most manufacturers of any significance bought an example to see how it was done, and the influence of the Traction can be seen in many well-known post-war designs.

The rear-wheel-drive Lancia Aprilia of 1936 was an Italian counterpart to the Citroën, and was the last and perhaps the finest of Vincenzo Lancia's achievements. Although more conservative

Maybach's awesome Zeppelin used an 8-liter engine. This is a 1934 car with cabriolet body.

than the bold Citroën, it had unitary construction, all-round independent suspension, and a typically Lancia narrow-V engine with four cylinders and single overhead camshaft; the only feature less than up to the moment was the unsynchronized gearbox. The fastback body with its wheel-at-each-corner design and pillarless construction was particularly striking, and incorporated some splendid Art Deco detailing.

Altogether more modest was the Fiat 500 of 1936, affectionately known as the Topolino after the Italian name for Walt Disney's Mickey Mouse. The smallest car in the world to be put into mass-production, the 569cc Fiat was a triumph of creative engineering that was arrived at in a slightly cock-eyed way: the body was designed first and then engineer Dante Giacosa had to work out how to fit the rear-wheel-drive mechanicals underneath it. Thus to squeeze an in-line four-cylinder engine under the sloping bonnet, Giacosa mounted it forward of the axle line and put the radiator behind the engine. As a result there was more interior room within the wheelbase. The chassis was a short and flimsy A frame, drilled extensively to save weight and only acquiring the necessary rigidity when the body was attached to it.

The end product was a nimble, cheerful little two-seater of surprising spaciousness and endearingly cheeky appearance. Over

Sober-bodied Rolls-Royce Phantom III has coachwork by Thrupp and Maberly. A 1938 model, it has been in the family of former racing driver Jack Sears since new.

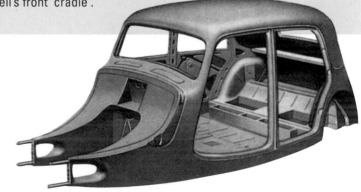

The monoque of the 1934 Traction Avant Citroën — at first it had structural problems, but was soon developed into a rigid heart for the car. The engine, gearbox and front suspension could be detached as one assembly from the prongs of the shell's front 'cradle'.

Lagonda's V12 was designed by W. O. Bentley. This 1938 model is a Rapide, with sporting drophead coachwork; an unusual feature for a car with wind-up windows is the fold-flat screen.

The Grosser Mercedes was the top model in the Stuttgart manufacturer's range. A 1931 model, this example was built for the former Kaiser William II and did not have the optional supercharger.

500,000 were built, from 1936 until 1955.

With such extremes as the pocket-sized Fiat and the battle-cruiser V16 Cadillac, the 1930s offered a more fascinating variety of models than almost any other decade, with the added excitement of a maturing industry coming to grips with new engineering solutions. The motor car was coming of age.

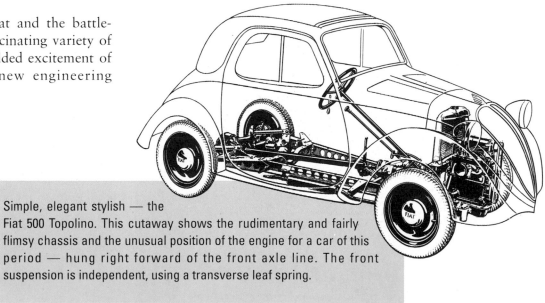

Simple, elegant stylish — the Fiat 500 Topolino. This cutaway shows the rudimentary and fairly flimsy chassis and the unusual position of the engine for a car of this period — hung right forward of the front axle line. The front suspension is independent, using a transverse leaf spring.

One of the greatest of pre-Second World War Mercedes models? The 540K is certainly hugely imposing in Special Roadster form, as here. Power from the overhead-valve straight-eight was 180bhp with the supercharger engaged.

Alfa Romeo's delectable 8C-2300. The body by
Touring of Milan has the distinctive tailfin of this
style. The supercharged straight-eight engine is a
masterpiece of design: note the characteristic
ribbed intake manifold.

This 2900 with sports
coachwork was both
designed and built by
Alfa Romeo. This
particular car ended up
in the United States of
America, where its
chassis was used for
one special and its
body for another.
However, the two were
reunited during the
1980s and the car was
fully restored.

Breathtakingly bodied by Touring,
this Alfa Romeo 8C-2900 is the
1938 Le Mans car of drivers
Sommer and Biondetti. It retired
when well in the lead, as the
result of a valve breakage.

Lancia's top model during this period was the V8-powered
Astura, of which this example carries drophead Pininfarina
coachwork from 1936-7. The engine is a 3-liter in this
instance, and the cruciform chassis uses Lancia's traditional
sliding-pillar front suspension.

The Bugatti Type 55 followed on from the Type 43 as a super-sports model derived from Bugatti grand prix cars. Introduced in 1932, it had a supercharged 2.3-liter straight-eight with twin overhead cams; power was around 130bhp, and the 0–60mph (0–100km/h) acceleration time was 13 seconds, according to a 1937 test by *The Autocar* magazine.

Bugatti's top tourer of the first half of the 1930s was the Type 50, introduced in 1930. Here it carries late-1930s coachwork by the British firm Abbott of Farnham. Again, power comes from a blown 2.3-liter twin-cam unit.

This Type 50, on the other hand, carries Jean Bugatti's distinctive *coupé profilé* bodywork, with its characteristic two-toning and steeply raked screen.

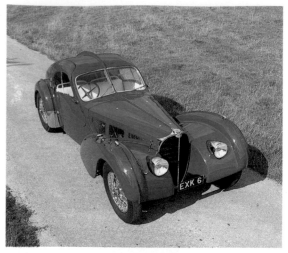

The most extraordinary bodywork of all on the Bugatti Type 57 was this Atlantic coupé, with its riveted external seams.

The catalogued coach two-door Delahaye has a simple elegance.

The French firm Delahaye bounced back in the mid-1930s with the Type 135. This 1938 car carries relatively restrained coachwork by Figoni et Falaschi, and has the sports MS engine.

An appreciably more flamboyant Delahaye is this Figoni et Falaschi design, created for an Indian client.

Another splendid French vehicle was the Delage D8, which had a 4-liter straight-eight. Coachwork was invariably elegant and this 1930 example with body by Henri Chapron was no exception.

A Figoni et Falaschi creation, but this time on a Talbot-Lago chassis. This style of teardrop-shaped coupé was used on quite a few Talbots.

Yet another Figoni et Falaschi product: this Talbot-Lago 150SS dates from 1937–8. Being an SS, it has a short-wheelbase chassis as well as the hemi-head engine, and is thus closely related to the Talbot-Lago competition cars. Like all cars of the marque from this period, it has a preselector gearbox.

Styles other than the Speedster were offered on
the Auburn. This is a cabriolet.

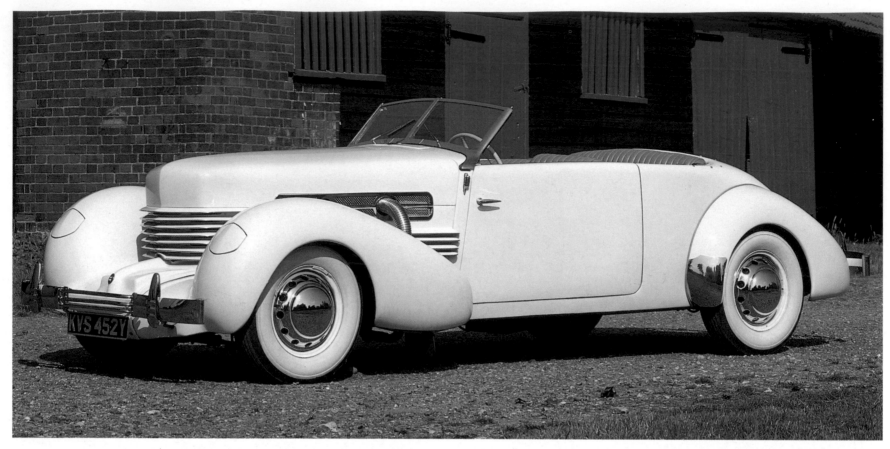

The dramatic supercharged Cord 812 had countless modern features, over and above its front-wheel drive, when it was announced in 1935. The 'coffin nose' and retractable headlamps are notable styling devices, and power comes from a 4730cc Lycoming V8.

Beauty out of improvisation: the Cord's job-lot switches and dials; note the miniature lever for actuating the electro-vacuum gearshift.

The revived Bentley produced under Rolls-Royce ownership was a fine sporting car. Shown is a 1939 4½-liter model with drophead bodywork by H.J. Mulliner.

The most stunning of all the 4½-liter Lagonda models was the Rapide, with its pointed tail, flared wings, and outside exhaust. The cars were developed by W. O. Bentley.

The 'low chassis' Type S Invicta was a spiritual successor to the 'W. O.' Bentleys. It was powered by a sturdy inline six of 4½ liters made by the British proprietary engine manufacturer Henry Meadows.

The British firm of Talbot (as opposed to the French Talbot-Lago enterprise)
was taken over in 1935 by the Rootes organization. This meant that the finely
engineered Talbots designed by Georges Roesch were gradually phased out.
This 1937 Talbot 75 is one of the last of the line.

The Alvis Speed 20 ultimately gave way to the 3½-liter Speed 25. This 1937 car carries typical four-door tourer coachwork.

Alvis produced fine British sporting cars. This 1932 Speed 20 has Vanden Plas drophead coupé coachwork, and is powered by a 2½-liter overhead-valve six. Later models had independent front suspension and an all-synchromesh gearbox.

The aristocrat of the prewar Alvis range was the 4.3-liter, good for 100mph (160km/h). The tourer body on this example is by Vanden Plas, who bodied many Alvis cars.

A sporting British thoroughbred from 1935: the Riley Sprite. Power comes from a 1496cc version of the famous four-cylinder twin-cam Riley engine, and there is a preselector gearbox.

The SS100 was available both as a 2½ liter and as a 3½ liter, both these engines were Standard-based, and Standard-built. The car was current from 1935 to 1939.

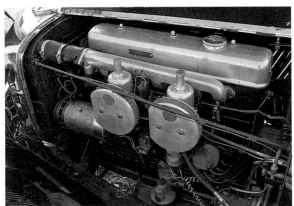

Seen here with one of its descendants, a Jaguar XJ-S cabriolet, is the splendidly styled SS Jaguar 100. In this car somewhat ordinary, but well-handled mechanicals were used , and they included the Standard six-cylinder engine in an ohv version.

The most modern of the prewar sports cars — and generally regarded as the finest, too. The BMW 328 combined elegant looks with a first-rate hemi-head engine and was much used by the competition fraternity both in its native Germany and in Britain.

The 327 was BMW's top prewar touring model, and carried two-seater coupé or cabriolet bodywork. Normally the engine was a 55bhp unit, but there was also a version with the tuned 80bhp 'hemi' from the 328. This is one of these desirable models, known as the 327/28.

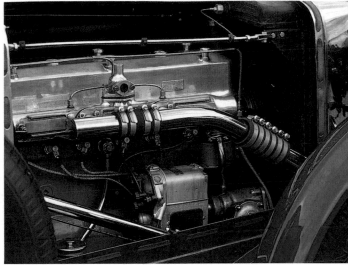

MG's giant-killing K3 Magnette: the small overhead-cam six of only 1087cc uses a supercharger to push power up to 120bhp; as on the 'blower' Bentley, the supercharger is positioned between the dumb irons. The black car is a replica, built from the mechanicals of an ordinary Magnette saloon of the period.

First of a great line — the M-type MG Midget, current from 1928 until 1932. Lightly modified Morris Minor mechanicals were underneath that rakish body, but that overhead-cam engine of 847cc had immense development potential.

A later Frazer Nash: a 1933 TT Replica model, powered by a 1½-liter Meadows engine. Production of 'Chain Gang' Frazer Nashes tailed off in 1936, although the last was made as late as 1939.

Another upper-crust British sports car: the Aston Martin Ulster. Powered by an overhead-cam 1495cc four-cylinder, it was a successful competition car and was manufactured between 1934 and 1936. This particular car finished 12th in the 1935 Le Mans.

More representative of roadgoing Aston Martins — although most were open cars — is this sports saloon of a type produced between 1934 and 1935. Again, the power unit is a 1½-liter four-cylinder.

A design classic: the Traction Avant Citroën. This is a 1956 model, an Onze Légère in French terminology; the Onze Normale is longer and wider. The Citroën was current from 1934 until 1957.

Extremely desirable is this cabriolet version of the Traction Avant, as it was only made before the Second World War. This is a British-assembled version — these always had chromed radiator shells. The special Pilote wheels on this example were introduced for 1938 and disappeared in 1946; they are much sought-after today.

Lancia stuck with rear-wheel drive for its otherwise advanced Aprilia. Power came from a narrow configured V4, of 1352cc until 1939 and thereafter of 1486cc. A platform chassis was offered to coachbuilders, but the factory-made Aprilia had an integral body/chassis.

The Fiat 500 or Topolino was a charming small car with advanced engineering. This is a pre-Second World War model with the original flathead engine. In 1948 the Fiat received overhead valves, and a year later it was restyled with a flat front. This is only a two-seater, although the post-war station wagons seat four.

4

From War to Boom

The Second World War held back automotive development for some years; proof, if needed, comes from the fact that it took the powerful United States motor industry until the 1949 model year fully to replace its prewar designs. The war also led ultimately to the demise of some of the finest marques, notably in France.

Adapt or die

Bugatti, Delahaye, Delage and Talbot-Lago all proved unable to adapt to changed circumstances, in a new world where — the United States apart — there was a limited market for super-expensive luxury cars. In the last burst of French specialist coachbuilding, however, cars of these marques were seen carrying bodies of an extraordinary if not always well-judged elegance: the 'greats' seemed determined to go down in style, and the French *carrossiers*, grappling to reconcile streamlined modern shapes with more traditional forms in their designs, rose to the challenge.

Ironically, it was Bugatti, the most renowned of the great marques, that showed the greatest willingness to move with the times: at the 1947 Paris motor show the company displayed a new 1488cc four-cylinder model, the Type 73. The styling of the teardrop-shaped coupé was hardly modern, and there was a beam front axle, but the Type 73 had the potential to relaunch Bugatti as a producer of small high-efficiency sporting cars.

However, Ettore Bugatti had unfortunately died in August

Last of the line: the Type 101 Bugatti was launched at the 1951 Paris motor show and was nothing more than a revived pre-Second World War Type 57. Only six — possibly seven — were made.

that year, and his family proved unable to restart car manufacture at the Molsheim plant — although in the early 1950s a few examples of a Type 101 model were turned out. These were essentially warmed-over Type 57s, and were hopelessly outdated as well as rather ugly.

Delahaye entered the postwar era in seemingly sound health, thanks to the fine reputation of its 3½-liter 135 range. Unfortunately the firm over reached itself, launching an upmarket 4½-liter series in 1946. These proved to have disappointing road behaviour and questionable reliability, and were withdrawn in 1951. Despite this, Delahaye retained a high profile, thanks to its being the principal supplier of bare chassis to French coachbuilders.

Some truly stunning 135s and 4½-liter 178s resulted, voluptuous chrome-bedecked extravagances for the privileged few. In 1951 came a new 3½-liter model, the 235, but this triple-carb 150bhp grand tourer failed to revive the company's fortunes, and barely 80 examples were built before Delahaye production ceased in 1954.

Sister marque Delage appeared to have lost any sense of purpose in these years. The prewar eight-cylinder models were not reintroduced, and the firm had to rely on a stodgy 3-liter six, which generally received singularly uninspiring bodywork. The last Delages were made in 1953.

Talbot-Lago fought longer and harder than either Delage or Delahaye, as Antony Lago built on his prewar policy of developing road and competition models in parallel. In 1946 he announced a new 4½-liter model with twin high-set camshafts in the style of the Riley. As a competition car it could contest the latest 4½-liter Formula One series, while as the Lago-Record it was a potent road car. Despite a hefty and essentially prewar chassis, the Lago-Record was good for 105mph (170km/h) and the factory-listed coachwork continued to be elegant and restrained — at least until the prewar sedan and drophead styles were replaced by a clumsy-looking pontoon-form sedan in 1951.

Alongside the Record, Talbot offered the short-wheelbase Lago Grand Sport, a successor to the prewar Lago SS. Built on a new design of chassis, it used a big-valve alloy cylinder head with a raised compression ratio: power was 190bhp, sufficient for up to 120mph (193km/h). Most Grand Sports went to outside coachbuilders, and some spectacular bodies resulted — as well as some that were predictably ghastly.

Only 36 Grand Sports were made before Lago decided to offer a cheaper factory-built model to pull in more sales. The new 1953–4 Grand Sport had a smart modern coupé body and a 210bhp engine, but remained overpriced and overweight: 3640lb (1650kg) as against 2654lb (1204kg) for the Aston Martin DB2-4. Few were sold.

The 4½-liter Talbots were hardly money spinners for the company, and Lago's competition program was a further drain on the firm's resources. An ill-judged four-cylinder model launched in 1949 was not the answer, and so Talbot retrenched and introduced a new coupé as its sole model for 1955. This had a lightweight tubular chassis and a revised 2½-liter version of the twin-cam four-cylinder which Lago had evolved from his 4½-liter six. The body was a shrunken version of the 1953–4 Grand Sport coupé, and was much lighter; also the traditional Wilson preselector gearbox was

Figoni et Falaschi and Saoutchik vied with each other to provide the most flamboyant coachwork on the Delahaye chassis. This outlandish creation is by Figoni et Falaschi.

replaced by a conventional synchromesh unit.

It was a brave try, but the new car was still too costly for what it offered. After 54 had been made it was re-engined with a BMW V8, but by 1959 it was all over for Talbot. The last five cars were ignominiously fitted with the Simca V8 engine — which was nothing more than a French-built Ford flathead. It was a sad end to a fine marque.

It was those manufacturers who adapted to the needs of a

new and poorer Europe who survived. Panhard was a classic example. Before the war it offered a range of bizarrely styled luxury cars with sleeve-valve engines. These would have been totally unsaleable in the 1940s, so Panhard took the bold step of adopting the ultra-lightweight aluminium-hulled economy car designed during the war by the idiosyncratic but talented French engineer Jean-Albert Grégoire.

The result was the 1946 front-wheel-drive Dyna. Aluminium-panelled but without the Grégoire's expensive cast-alloy hull, it evolved into the extraordinary Dyna 54 of 1953. At the time this was the most advanced family sedan in the world. Built as an all-aluminium monocoque, this streamlined six-seater Panhard weighed only 1443lb (650kg) and was good for 75mph (120km/h) despite its modest 851cc flat-twin power unit. Such performance embarrassed more conventional rivals, but the cost of manufacturing the Dyna 54 was too high and so by 1956 it was wholly made of steel, with an inevitable weight penalty. The original alloy cars stand, however, as an important technical achievement that even today has not been bettered.

Despite the winds of utilitarianism, the days of the *grand routier* were not yet quite over in France, however, and a new manufacturer arose to take the place of the disappearing great marques. This was pressed-metal specialist and car-body manufacturer Facel. Building on its experience constructing coupé bodies for Ford-France and Simca, it came up in 1954 with a broad-shouldered and flashily detailed 2 + 2 powered by the 4½-liter Chrysler 'Firedome' V8.

Called the Facel-Vega, the new car had a simple chassis with a live rear axle suspended by leaf springs; with around 180bhp on tap, performance was most impressive. In 1958 the car became the HK500, with a 5.9-liter Chrysler V8 and a bold, stacked-headlamp front to complement the wraparound shield introduced in 1956.

It was an imposing vehicle, and soon attracted many celebrity customers. Some journalists have criticized the HK500 for having a chassis not up to the car's considerable power, but former owners such as racing driver Stirling Moss still speak highly of this stylish Franco-American. A four-door limousine joined the range in 1956, and the 'mini-Facel' four-cylinder Facellia in 1959.

The sun sets for the British coachbuilder

In Britain, meanwhile, car development progressed cautiously — although designs such as the flat-four Jowett Javelin stood out for their modernity. As the industry moved over to unitary construction, however, one trend was clear: the gradual disappearance of the specialist coachbuilder. On the way, though, there were some splendid last-gasp exercises, most notably on the conservative but well-engineered Daimler chassis.

Dominating this niche was Daimler-owned Hooper, who came up with the swoopy Empress body seen on various different sizes of Daimler during this period. The firm was also responsible for the outrageous 'Docker Daimlers', flamboyantly trimmed show

cars built for Daimler boss Dudley Docker and his wife.

Meanwhile, Rolls-Royce again demonstrated deft footwork by moving away from the super-expensive prewar cars and majoring on a 4¼-liter model with a standardized pressed-steel body. Generally sold as a Bentley, designated the Mk VI, this spawned the much-coveted fastback Continental, a beautifully mannered grand tourer with a mildly uprated engine.

The Mk VI evolved into the 4½-liter R-type, which in 1955 gave way to the new pontoon-bodied Bentley S1 and Rolls-Royce Silver Cloud. In 1959 these received a V8 engine supposedly inspired by the Cadillac power unit. These fine cars were emphatically owner-driver sedans, in contrast to the limited-production Silver Wraith limousines.

Equally exclusive but altogether more sporting were the early Bristols, built by the Bristol Aeroplane Co and derived from the prewar BMW. The aerodynamically efficient 401 and 403 coupés were beautifully crafted cars of undoubted engineering quality, offering relaxed high-speed cruising despite their modest 2-liter engine.

The same BMW-based power unit was used for the postwar Frazer Nash sports cars, which were high-grade limited-production models intended mainly for competition use; fewer than 200 were built, and today they are much valued.

In the United States, technology took a back seat to ever more extravagant styling. Engine design forged ahead, however, with the V8 becoming widespread during the 1950s, along with automatic transmission and power steering. The rise of the V8 in fact led to something of a horsepower race, a phenomenon that brought Chrysler to the fore.

The Hemi of 1951 was indeed a great achievement by Chrysler, being capable of 352bhp with minimal tuning and of around 1000bhp when modified for drag racing. It led to the first of the so-called muscle cars, the 300bhp 1955 Chrysler 300, produced a Chrysler domination of NASCAR racing in the United States, and powered the Cunningham that came 3rd in the 1953 Le Mans.

Delahaye's last gasp, the Type 235. It was essentially an uprated 135, and retained the earlier car's transverse-leaf independent front suspension and conventional semi-elliptic rear. Various coachbuilders bodied the chassis; this one is again by Chapron.

The fabulous Ferrari

In direct opposition to cluttered American efforts were the clean lines evolved by Italian stylist Pininfarina, who pioneered the European fastback with his 1948 Cisitalia and went on to present the pure, elegant Lancia Aurelia Gran Turismo coupé.

Powered by an elegant alloy V6 of initially only 1754cc, the fastback Aurelia was the car that created the modern GT genre. Current until 1958, it featured a rear-mounted clutch and gearbox, and rear suspension at first by semi-trailing arms and later by De Dion axle. Competition successes were not slow in coming, and the Aurelia is today an undoubted classic.

The Lancia, however, was overshadowed by an altogether more magical Italian newcomer: the Ferrari. Very much an equivalent to the prewar Bugatti in its character, the Ferrari was in the same way bred for competition, and designed under the aegis of a similarly inspired company chief.

The first Ferrari was the 125 of May 1947. At its heart was a jewel-like 1497cc all-alloy V12 built around a seven-bearing crank machined from a solid billet of steel, and with two chain-driven overhead camshafts and a twin-coil ignition system. The simple but strong chassis was made of oval-section manganese-chrome tubing and was cruciform-braced.

Two jumps in engine size by the end of 1947 saw the Ferrari with a capacity of 1995cc and a new model designation of 166. The following year the new marque won its first victories in the Mille

It was big, and it seated six, but this Panhard Dyna 54 weighed only 1443lb (650kg), and was powered by an 851cc flat-twin unit. Streamlining and a lightweight aluminium bodyshell were the secret.

Miglia and Targa Florio. It won the same events again in 1949, and also came in 1st at Le Mans. Ferrari had begun as it was to continue, initiating a process of cross-pollination between road cars and competition models that was to lead to some of the greatest race-bred grand tourers of the post-Second World War years.

The Ferrari 166 evolved through 195 and 212 models before being replaced by the 3-liter 250 Europa in 1953. In 1951 an additional touring model had been introduced, a 4.1-liter powered by a new engine derived from that of the Ferrari GP car. Called the 340 America, this received a 4½-liter engine in 1953 and was renamed the 375 America.

At this stage Enzo Ferrari was feeling his way as a manufacturer of touring cars, and by 1954 had made fewer than 200 Ferraris for the road — as against 250 competition models. The touring Ferraris were bodied by various Italian coachbuilders, and no two were identical: this was bespoke manufacture at its finest. The 250GT of 1954 changed all this. A new short-wheelbase chassis brought in coil-spring front suspension and enhanced roadholding, the 2953cc engine was based on the original Ferrari 125 V12 rather than the heftier 340 unit, and Pininfarina bodied the

Superb coupé coachwork on this original-series 1948 short-wheelbase Talbot-Lago Grand Sport is a one-off by Chapron.

cars in a taut muscular style evolved from his brutal but elegant competition Ferrari coupés. As that hackneyed phrase has it, aptly in this case, a legend had been born.

The coupé 250GT was eventually joined by a cabriolet and in 1959 by the limited-production Spyder California, a more sporting open model, Meanwhile in 1958 Pinin Farina had come out with new sharp-edged styling for the regular coupé and cabriolet. These 250GTs were the series-production Ferraris: seductive machines with a spine-tingling, howling, carved-from-the-solid V12 unit and firm, instant responses in perfect harmony with that magnificent power plant.

For those who wanted something more exclusive, the bigger Ferraris continued, with the 375 America giving way to the 410 Super America in 1956. Only 14 of the 410SA were built, for customers such as the Shah of Iran and the Emperor of Indo-China, and coachwork was frequently dramatic.

Maserati lagged behind Ferrari as a manufacturer of touring cars. Its small sixes of 1947–57 were fine cars, especially the 1985cc twin-cam A6G-2000 announced in 1954, but it took the potent 3500GT of 1957 and the later and ultra-rare V8-powered 5000GT to push the Bologna company into the limelight.

This cutaway drawing shows the Spyder Corsa racing version of the Ferrari 166. Clearly visible is the cruciform-braced tubular chassis characteristic of early Ferraris. The rear suspension is by simple semi-elliptics.

German rivals: Porsche and Mercedes

In West Germany, the premier sporting marque was a new one: Porsche. Production of the company's first model, the 356, began in 1948, and the little VW-powered streamlined coupé soon became popular in competition.

It was not long in moving away from its Volkswagen Beetle roots, and in 1951 a 1500cc engine with a roller-bearing crank became available for racing. A year later a plain-bearing road 1500 arrived, and the Porsche 356 was well on the way to maturity as a civilized and crisp mini-GT of delightful delicacy and precision — and with excellent roadholding and handling, providing you took account of its rear engine and did not provoke it into potentially uncontrollable oversteer.

The 356 continued until 1965, with the Carrera the most coveted model. This used a version of the dry-sump twin-plug engine from the racing 550, a hideously complex unit with a roller-bearing crank and with quad cams driven by shaft and bevel.

Unsurprisingly, Mercedes eventually re-entered motor sport, and from its Le Mans-winning sports-racing coupé of 1952 the firm developed the legendary 1954 gullwing 300SL. To offset the weight of the heavy 3-liter engine from the 300 sedan, Mercedes built the SL around a lightweight tubular spaceframe. This made the door sills so high that the only way to ensure adequate access

was to use gullwing top-hinged doors cut into the roof. The running gear was essentially as the 300 sedan, but the 195bhp engine had dry-sump lubrication and fuel injection — for the first time on a production car.

The 300SL was good for up to 161mph (259km/h), but the traditional Mercedes swing-axle rear gave unpredictable handling, while the massive finned aluminium drum brakes were not fully up to slowing such a fast and heavy car. In 1957 the gullwing Mercedes was discontinued in favour of a convertible model with orthodox doors and a cleverly re-engineered and much improved swing axle.

Twin cams and British Racing Green

In Britain, too, there was a new sporting 'great': the Jaguar. With its XK120 of 1948, the company launched the world's first mass-produced twin-overhead-cam engine. Not only that, but the all-enclosed bodywork of the XK120 was of breathtaking grace and made the Jaguar a highly popular export to the United States. The superb 3442cc XK straight-six gave the Coventry firm the power unit to match its sporting aspirations, and was a key element in the successful C and D type racers that between them notched up five Le Mans victories. At the same time the engine demonstrated its versatility by propelling the luxurious Mk VII sedan to over 100mph (160km/h). Thanks to such achievements, backed up by the launch of the compact 2.4 model in 1955, Jaguar became the world's premier quantity manufacturer of sporting cars.

Also successful in sports car racing, although to a lesser degree, was Aston Martin, which established a new marque identity with its DB series. The original DB2 of 1949 was an amalgam of an Aston chassis with a Lagonda twin-cam engine designed by W. O. Bentley, and followed the merger of the two firms in 1947. The chassis was well considered, and featured a firmly

There was also a four-door Facel, the Excellence. Introduced in 1956, it had pillarless construction, resulting in questionable rigidity. Only 152 were made, all but five with the wraparound shield and sharp tailfins shown here.

Jaguar's XK engine of 1948 was the first power unit to be designed by the Coventry firm, and has proved a rugged, versatile and long-lived unit. An in-line six, it has an iron block and an alloy cylinder head.

located coil-sprung live back axle; the six-cylinder 2580cc engine developed 125bhp in tuned Vantage form, and the fastback bodywork was pleasing to the eye.

Throughout the 1950s the Aston evolved steadily, and in 1958 came a new model, the beautifully smooth-lined DB4. It was constructed according to the Italian coachbuilder Touring's *Superleggera* method in which aluminium panelling was attached to a lightweight tubular frame, and was powered by a new all-alloy twin-cam. Without a doubt it was Britain's finest grand tourer.

Sporting favourites

Of more general relevance, however, was the blossoming of the British sports car, with Austin-Healey, MG and Triumph, along with Jaguar, all becoming big export earners for Britain.

The Austin-Healey won friends for its rakish styling, which somehow eclipsed its humdrum Austin running gear, and the hybrid marque bolstered its reputation through an impressive showing in competition both in Europe and in the United States. The cheeky little 'Frogeye' Sprite was another success, and pioneered the revival of the cheap 'starter' sports car.

MG faltered in the early 1950s, as corporate politics at BMC, the parent company, left the firm too long with the outdated 'square-rigger' models. But with the TF replaced by the modern MGA, the marque re-established itself in the all-important Amercian market, and went on to develop the potent MGA Twin-Cam — unfortunately too demanding in its engineering to be reliable in insensitive hands.

A British Lancia? The Jowett Javelin of 1946-52 was Britain's most advanced family sedan during this period, with an ohv flat-four engine, supple torsion-bar suspension all-round (with a live rear axle), and an aerodyamically efficient integral-construction body. Poor reliability, and a relatively high price, scuppered this brave endeavour, but today the Jowett is much coveted.

As for Triumph, its success story was the TR, which was again based on modest mechanicals but proved robust, and effective in competition. These may not have been 'greats', but they were certainly important cars.

Compared to the stunning little Lotus Elite of 1957, however, cars such as the TRs and the Austin-Healeys seemed like trucks. The Elite was an extraordinary achievement: a fiberglass monocoque of impressive aerodynamic efficiency, powered by a lightweight Coventry-Climax engine that gave the 1512lb (686kg) Lotus a power-to-weight ratio the equal of many bigger cars. Unfortunately the pioneering grp structure posed many problems, some of the engineering solutions were half-baked, and refinement and reliability were fairly abysmal. Brave and beautiful, the Elite was the saddest cul-de-sac in British sports car design during the 1950s. If only execution had matched concept...

Also bodied in fiberglass was the Chevrolet Corvette, America's attempt to produce a sports car of its own. As introduced in 1953 it was a fairly crude device, with a simple cruciform chassis, a tuned version of the 3.8-liter Chevrolet 'Stovebolt Six' — and automatic transmission.

It was a lemon, and General Motors nearly axed it when faced with minimal sales. However, the arrival of V8 power for 1955 was followed by a new manual-shift option and then by a restyle and chassis tweak-up for 1956. After this, continuous honing of the design and progressive power increases gradually turned the Corvette into a serious sports car with performance to match its looks — especially in 290bhp fuel-injected form.

Modern design for the modern world

The true greats of the 1950s were not, however, to be found among high-priced sports and GT cars, but rather in the sphere of popular motoring, where the decade saw some towering technical and commercial achievements.

The latter aspect was more relevant to the success of the Volkswagen Beetle. In engineering terms it was a dead end, with its air-cooled rear engine and platform chassis, but its high-quality construction, unrivalled reliability and excellent after-sales back-up made it a consumer durable without parallel: it was a superb tool, and a spiritual descendant of the Ford Model T it eventually outsold.

The Citroën 2CV was another oddball, only even more so, but again it had an extraordinary fitness for purpose.

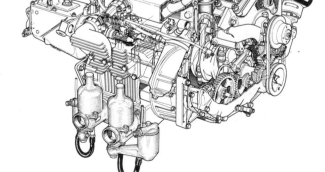

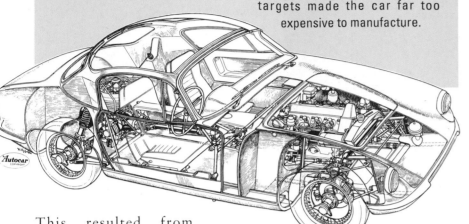

The Lotus Elite of 1957 was a pioneering fiberglass monocoque. Its structure caused many problems not least when rigid weight targets made the car far too expensive to manufacture.

Rolls-Royce made an astute move when in 1946 it offered its first car with a standardized body: the Bentley Mk VI. This is the later 1952-5 R-type version, with a bigger trunk and the 4½-liter engine introduced in 1951. Behind is the Rolls-Royce version, the Silver Dawn.

This resulted from sparking lateral thinking by a design team unrestrained by convention. Intended to be a simple idiot-proof economy car to motorize the French farmer, it had ingenious interconnected suspension to cope with poor French roads, a 375cc air-cooled twin deliberately restricted to 9bhp, and a minimalist body bristling with clever features.

In comparison, Britain's equally loved Morris Minor seemed the spirit of conservatism, although it was in fact an extremely well-executed design that enjoyed roadholding and handling unequalled in the small car class. The continuing worldwide affection for the durable and friendly Minor testifies to its excellence, as do its substantial sales over 23 years of manufacture.

Then there was the Citroën DS, almost as revolutionary as the Traction Avant Citroën had been in its day. With its hydropneumatic system providing self-levelling variable-rate suspension and actuating the brakes, assisting the steering, and operating the clutch and gear change, the 1955 DS was a technical tour de force even before you took into account its styling and its base-unit body construction. That the car was still competitive when replaced 20 years on by the CX is testament enough to its place in history.

The same can be said of Alec Issigonis's Mini, which is perhaps the best example of how greatness has nothing to do with size or cost: it is all down to the quality of the vehicle's design.

Daimler made too many models in too few numbers to be able to survive in the post-Second World War years. A popular style on the Daimler chassis was the Empress design by Hooper, with its razor-edge cabin and swooping wing line. Most were four-door cars, but this 3½-liter model has two-door coachwork.

Introduced in 1955, the replacements for the Silver Dawn and the R-type were the Rolls-Royce Silver Cloud and the Bentley S-type. Mechanically they were much as before at first, but in 1959 came an alloy V8 of 6230cc. Shown here is a Silver Cloud II with this power unit.

With the Mini, Issigonis proved that an ultra-compact front-wheel-drive car using an orthodox in-line four-cylinder engine was technically feasible. The secret was to install the gearbox and final drive in the sump.

However, he did not stop there: in terms of space saving, suspension design and overall functionalism, he created a unique package that has never been bettered, and which has been a very important influence on popular car design ever since its 1959 launch. As the herald of a new era of technological boundary pushing the Mini was without parallel.

Bristol's delightful aerodynamic 403 of 1953-5 together with a later 406. The 403 is an improved 100bhp version of the 85bhp 401 first seen in 1948. *Superleggera* construction is used, with an alloy body built over a lightweight steel-tube frame.

The postwar Frazer Nash used the BMW-derived Bristol engine, and was a high-priced connoisseur's sports car of which fewer than 200 were produced. This is the most desirable model of all, the Le Mans Replica.

One of the most legendary vehicles of all time, the Jeep. Once described as 'a divine instrument of military locomotion', it entered production in 1941 and was made in the United States by both Willys and Ford.

The first new postwar Studebaker range was styled by top industrial designer Raymond Loewy's studio, and the Starlight coupés featured a controversial panoramic rear window. This example also has the bullet nose introduced for 1950.

Another Studebaker, and another uncharacteristically clean
American design: again by the Loewy studio. The car is a
1955 President coupé, of a basic style introduced for the 1953
model year. The engine is a 3.8-liter V8.

A big styling influence: Pininfarina's simple and cleanly executed coupé for Cisitalia.

Staid early Ferrari 166, complete with Borrani's distinctive alloy-rimmed disc wheels. The body is by Stabilimenti Farina, run by Battista Pinin Farina's elder brother. The style imitates the latter's Cisitalia.

A brace of 166s. The car on the left has open barchetta bodywork by Touring, and a later 195 engine; it came 12th in the 1950 Targa Florio. On the right is the 1949 Paris motor show 166 Inter, with its coupé body again by Touring. The Aerlux plastic sunroof is correct for the car.

This Ferrari 225 carries bodywork designed by Michelotti and built by Vignale. Most 225 coupés had this style of body. The 225 was evolved from the preceding 212, and thus has the original short-block V12 engine.

The famous 250GT, the first of the series-built Ferrari models. This is a 1957 car of the type known as the Tour de France after its successes in this event. The 250GT was introduced in 1954 and has a 2953cc version of the 'small' Ferrari V12, in conjunction with a four-speed all-synchro gearbox and a new chassis with coil spring front suspension.

Stunning tightly drawn Pininfarina coachwork characterizes this 1953 Ferrari 250 MM, which is one of 19 such cars to have this style of body. The power output of the 2953cc long-block V12 with its three Weber carbs is 240bhp. The tubular chassis has the usual transverse-leaf front suspension and semi-elliptic rear.

A Ferrari 340, one of
the cars entered by the
factory in the 1952
Carrera Pan Americana
and fielded the following
year by American driver
Phil Hill. It is painted
in Hill's 1953 Carrera
colours.

The taut, well-proportioned bodywork on this 1955 Maserati A6G-2000 is by Allemano. Power came from a twin-plug dohc six and the chassis was made of oval tubes. Suspension was coil and wishbone at the front and quarter-elliptic at the rear.

Perfect muscular Pininfarina lines for a road/competition Ferrari: the short-wheelbase 250GT. This particular example is the car that won the 1960 Tourist Trophy race at Goodwood, driven by Stirling Moss.

This 1957 Maserati 3500GT carries coachwork by Pietro Frua, typical of his style. The engine was still a double-ohc six with twin plugs per cylinder, but the capacity was 3485cc and the output an alleged 220bhp.

California Spyder: a more hard-edged convertible
250GT than Ferrari's mainstream Pininfarina spyder, it
was intended for both road and track, and was current
between 1957 and 1962. For 1960 it was given the
chassis of the 250GT short-wheelbase coupé.

Porsche 356A coupé, as introduced in 1955. The one-piece windshield distinguishes it from the earlier 356s (the type dated back to 1948), and the flat-four engines used were a 1300 and a 1600, either with plain bearings or, for competition use, with roller bearings.

Journalist and Porsche writer Mike McCarthy enjoying a 1956 356A cabriolet. The 356A benefited from various suspension modifications to cut down oversteer.

Mercedes 300SL gullwing. With its fuel-injected engine — canted over 40 degrees from vertical — it was good for 0–60mph (0–100km/h) in around 8.5 seconds. The body is in steel, with alloy doors, hood and trunk.

The most famous Jaguar XK of all: NUB 120, the
XK120 extensively campaigned with in rallies by Ian
Appleyard. In 1952 it was the first car to win the
Coupe d'Or for completing the Alpine Rally three
times in succession without penalties.

Roadster Jaguar XK150: discs all round, tuned S engine optional, and a choice of either a 3.4- or a 3.8-liter unit from late 1959.

The follow-up to the XK120 was the XK140, identifiable by the coarser slatting of the grille and by the bigger bumpers. There was more power, plus rack-and-pinion steering. Behind is the subsequent Jaguar XK150, in drophead form. It was current from 1957 until 1961.

Thinly disguised race car: the Jaguar XK-SS was devised as a
way of disposing of unsaleable D types by kitting them up with
rudimentary road equipment. Only 16 were built.

GREAT CARS OF THE WORLD

A cut-price Bentley? The big Jaguar sedans offered an extraordinary combination of sporting performance and indulgent luxury. In the foreground is the M version of the Mk VII, with power from the XK engine up to 190bhp. Behind are a Mk VIII and a Mk IX, visually identical and recognizable by their one-piece windshields.

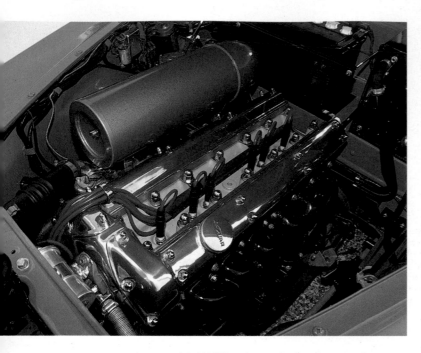

Jaguar chief William Lyons insisted on a twin-cam engine not just for performance and image but also for its aesthetic appeal: this shot of the Mk VIIM's power unit shows how admirably this aim was achieved.

An Aston Martin DB4 coupé shows off its elegant lines. But this is no ordinary DB: it is a short-wheelbase lightweight DB4GT.

The world's most durable and versatile workhorse, the four-wheel-drive aluminium-bodied Land-Rover. It was introduced in 1948; this is a short wheelbase Series I model, current until 1958.

Triple SU carburetors on this Aston Martin Vantage 266bhp engine.

The cheeky original Austin-Healey Sprite of 1958-61, nicknamed the 'Frogeye' in Britain and the 'Bugeye' in the United States. Mechanicals came from the Austin A35, but the steering was Morris Minor rack and pinion and the rear suspension was by quarter-elliptics.

The Austin-Healey 100: Austin A90 Atlantic mechanicals and a part-aluminium body. The engine is a 2660cc four-cylinder. Current from 1952 until 1956, the 100 had a three-speed gearbox with overdrive until 1955, and thereafter a four-speed unit with overdrive as an option.

A one-piece hood provided easy access to the 948cc BMC A series engine used in the Austin-Healey Sprite.

In 1956 the Austin-Healey received the 2639cc six-cylinder Austin engine, and became the 100 Six. The new car was heavier, slower, and handled less well, but was progressively improved over subsequent years. In its final 3000 Mk III form it was a civilized if somewhat vintage 150bhp sports convertible.

The very image of the British sports car? The perfectly proportioned upright MG TC was a descendant of the 1936 TA model, and used Morris components in a simple ladder chassis. The engine was a 1250cc four derived from the unit used in the 1938–48 Morris Ten.

The TC's successor, the MG TD of 1949–53. It had an all-new chassis with independent front suspension and steering by rack. The smaller disc wheels are a distinguishing point. Behind the TD in this illustration are first an HRG and then a Jowett Jupiter.

The MG TC was current from 1945 to 1949 with a total of 10,000 made. A great number of them were exported to the United States — despite having harsh beam-axle front suspension and being available only with right-hand drive.

Triumph's 1950s sporting contender, the TR. This is a
TR3A, recognizable by its 'dollar grin' full-width grille.
Mechanically straightforward, the 'cutaway door'
TRs were current from 1953 until 1962. They were
powered by a formidable 2-liter or 2.2-liter four.

A side view shows off to best effect the beautiful lines of the Lotus Elite. The fragile and troublesome pioneering fiberglass monocoque GT used Coventry-Climax's single-ohc 1216cc power unit.

The T type was finally replaced in 1955 by the MGA. Shown is the short-lived Twin-Cam version, with its potent 1588cc engine. This 108bhp power unit was intended to revive the notion of the special high-performance MG engine. But early examples gave many problems, and to be reliable the car demanded more attention in its driving and maintenance than the average owner demonstrated.

Classic and Sportscar magazine re-created one of the great 1950s sports car rivalries: Chevrolet Corvette versus Jaguar XK. The Jaguar is an XK140 and the Corvette a 1956 model, the year when things really began to come together for the Chevrolet.

A shape that needs no introduction. This
Volkswagen Beetle is one of the 'oval window'
models, as produced from 1953 to 1957.

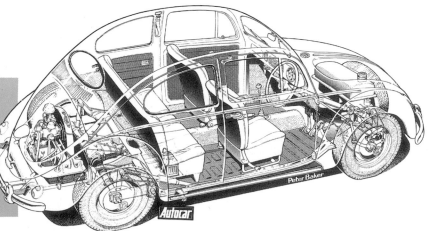

This view of the Volkswagen Beetle shows
the car's platform chassis and torsion-bar
suspension front and back — as well as
the rear-mounted air-cooled flat-four
so central to the VW's concept.

The Citroën 2 CV's air-cooled flat twin engine has its power deliberately restricted, and there is an oil cooler to allow foot-to-floor driving. The 2CV has front-wheel drive, of course.

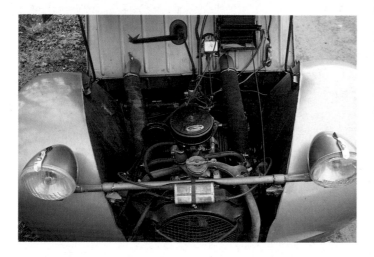

Citroën's technical and stylistic *tour de force*, the DS, made its European competition look rather old-fashioned. Here a British-assembled DS poses with a Rover 90 and a white Mercedes 190.

Citroën's DS stunned the motoring world when introduced in 1955. Its key feature was a high pressure hydropneumatic system which provided the car's springing and activated the brakes, steering and gearshift. The aerodynamic body was built around a unitary cage.

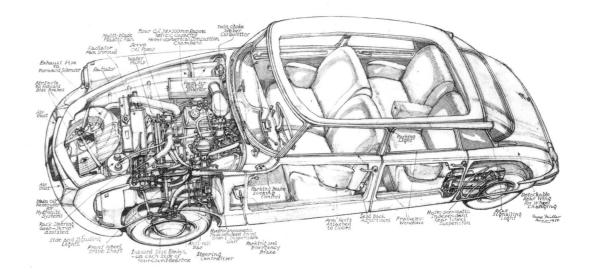

The Citroën 2CV, which went into production in the late 1940s, was created for French rural use, and was intended to displace the horse and cart. The grey car displays the roll-up canvas trunk cover used on early 2CV's; the red example is a British-assembled model with a metal trunk lid.

Britain's most-loved car, the
Morris Minor, made from 1948 to
the early 1970s. This photo shows
every body style and every model
series, with the original 'low-light'
sedan of 1948 in the forefront. At
first the Minor had the flathead
engine of the preceding Morris
Eight, but this was soon displaced
by a pushrod Austin unit.

GREAT CARS OF THE WORLD

A masterpiece of design in every aspect, the Mini of 1959 truly broke new ground. The exposed body seams are a typical detail and these, with the mono sides of the original cars, made the Mini virtually self-jigging on the production line.

The Mini's secret: transverse installation of the A series BMC engine.

Jaguar's first unitary construction car was the 2.4 sedan introduced in 1955. A 3.4 variant followed, and in 1959 the range was restyled and refined to become the much-loved Mk 2 series. This is a 2.4 Mk 1, with its smaller glass area and full wheel spats.

Shelby-Mustang GT350 in American racing colours. The additional quarter-
windows are a feature of the 1966 model year cars. The Shelby's hot 289 V8
delivers an honest 306bhp, and the suspension and brakes are uprated over
the standard Mustang's.

Speed and muscle

Performance became an ever more important attribute in the 1960s, not least as a result of the V8-led speed culture that grew up in the United States. This received a great fillip with the arrival of the so-called pony cars, the sporting Ford Mustang and its General Motors rivals, the Chevrolet Camaro and Pontiac Firebird.

Ponies and wild horses

The Mustang and the Camaro/Firebird were rather ordinary machines of no real engineering distinction: they were essentially 'image' cars for the young and prosperous products of the post-Second World War baby boom, and were based on prosaic mechanicals. However, both ranges spawned powerful competition-orientated variants that developed a considerable following.

Ford's version was the 4.7-liter Shelby-Mustang GT350. Created by high-profile Texan race driver Carroll Shelby, it dominated its class in SCCA (Sports Car Club of America) competition. Subsequent versions used a 7-liter 428. General Motors fielded a Z-28 version of the Camaro in riposte to the Shelby, and this 5-liter road-racing package delivered Chevrolet two SCCA championships, in 1968 and 1969. Pontiac, meanwhile, came up with the Firebird Trans Am, powered by a 335bhp 6.5-liter V8.

In early 1970 both GM ranges were restyled, becoming heavier and flabbier, a process the Mustang was also undergoing. Muscle was turning to fat, and with the beginning of the 1970s the golden years of the American pony car were drawing to an end.

Grifo, with aluminium panels riveted to this frame. Two Le Mans appearances followed, and from 1966 Bizzarrini produced the car under his own name. A total of around 140 were built.

The Iso bodies were designed at Bertone by a young stylist who is today one of the world's most respected names in this field, Giorgio Giugiaro. He was also responsible for the lines of another V8-powered GT of the era, the British Gordon-Keeble.

Mechanically the Gordon-Keeble was much as the Iso, with a Corvette 327 engine, a coil-and-wishbone front end, and a De Dion rear. This was probably no accident: the financier backing the Gordon-Keeble tried to interest Renzo Rivolta in making the car, and a prototype chassis was sent over to Italy. It returned covered in scribe marks; a little while later, out came the Iso Rivolta...

The fiberglass Gordon-Keeble was a well-equipped four-seater sold at a surprisingly modest price, and it received favourable reviews in the motoring press after its 1964 launch. Regrettably, the project was under-capitalized, and there were also problems with parts supply. Production finally ceased in 1966, after only 99 cars had been built.

Rather more successful was the oddly styled Jensen CV-8, launched in 1962 as a replacement for the Austin-powered 541 model with its hefty four-liter lorry engine. The CV-8 substituted for this the Chrysler V8, initially in 5.9-liter form. The rest of the running gear was much as before, with a simple leaf-

Pontiac's ponycar, the Firebird. This is a 1968 car, with the biggest engine then available, the 6½-liter 400. Brakes were drums all-round...

American power, European style

In Europe the American V8 offered a new field of opportunity for the specialist manufacturers, and following the example of the Facel-Vega a new breed of American-powered GTs sprang up.

Among the newcomers was the Italian firm Iso, which came out in 1962 with an elegant Bertone-styled coupé powered by the Chevrolet Corvette 5.4-liter V8. With a De Dion rear axle, the Iso Rivolta was a civilized car that generally handled well, but it was rather eclipsed by the more dramatic Grifo built on a shortened version of the same chassis. Entering production in 1965, the Grifo had fluid Bertone lines and less weight to carry around, and tended also to have a more powerful engine; the result was a 160mph (257km/h) grand tourer with immense performance and gratifying refinement. From 1972 a 7-liter version was offered.

A rather different device was born of the same parentage: the Iso Grifo A3C, also known as the Bizzarrini 5300GT. Intended as a racing version of the Grifo, it was created by Rivolta and Grifo designer Giotto Bizzarrini — who had previously been responsible for the Ferrari GTO, and in part for the Lamborghini V12 engine. A no-nonsense racing GT, the Grifo A3C used a multi-tube frame rather than the steel punt of the regular

The Corvette comes up to date: the 1963 model year saw the Chevrolet sports car not only restyled but also re-engineered. Primarily this involved a move to independent rear suspension, using transverse-leaf springing.

sprung rear, and the body was an adaptation of the 541's pioneering fiberglass shell.

The well-developed chassis gave impressive roadholding and handling, with a firm but not harsh ride, and the carefully appointed cockpit had many pleasing details; performance, needless to say, was more than sufficient. Unfortunately, the slant-eyed front-end design was bizarre in the extreme, and attracted much unfavourable comment. This led Jensen to go abroad for the styling of the CV-8's successor, and accordingly the steel-bodied Interceptor of 1966 emerged with lines by Touring. Now blessed with eye-catching good looks, the Jensen in its new form was a relaxed high-performance grand tourer of very real ability.

More intriguing, though, was a sister car introduced at the same time, the Jensen FF. This featured four-wheel drive by Ferguson, experts in this field, with a centre differential taking drive by chain to the output shaft for the front wheels. Along with this was anti-lock braking. The whole package was unprecedentedly advanced, and all the more a surprise for coming from a small British manufacturer such as Jensen.

The anti-lock brakes were not totally convincing, as they pulsed back badly through the pedal, but the four-wheel drive was phenomenal: the Jensen had 'almost unlimited traction and incredible roadholding', *Autocar* magazine wrote. The FF was a true technical landmark, but unfortunately it was not financially viable, and was eventually discontinued. Its mantle was ultimately

Smoothed out, but still identifiably a Facel-Vega: the last of the line, the Facel II of 1961–4. Its Chrysler V8 pushes out a claimed 390bhp.

picked up in 1980 by the Audi Quattro.

On a lower level the Ford V8 gave shattering performance to two seemingly improbable hybrids based on modestly engineered British sports cars. First off the line was the 1962 AC Cobra. Carroll Shelby recognized that putting the 'small block' Ford V8 in the AC Ace's tubular chassis would make a potent and appealing sports car for the American market, and he persuaded AC to go along with the idea. The result was the Cobra, which used the 4.2-liter Ford unit in an Ace with beefed-up chassis and four-wheel disc brakes. The Cobra was soon up-engined to 4.7 liters, and with Ford backing was developed for US racing.

More power was sought, however, and the obvious move was to fit Ford's 7-liter 'big block'. To make this feasible the chassis was redesigned, with out-of-hours Ford help. It ended up stiffer, three times stronger, and with coil-and-wishbone independent suspension all round, complete with anti-dive and anti-squat geometry and adjustable spherical joints.

The Iso Grifo's broad-shouldered good looks were the work of Bertone and the mechanicals were derived from the earlier Iso Rivolta. Power comes from a Chevrolet Corvette 5.4-liter V8 unit.

The Gordon-Keeble is one of those sad 'nearly' cars that could so easily have been a great. But production ended before a hundred had been made, and before imperfections in the car's steering could be resolved.

GREAT CARS OF THE WORLD

You can see the family likeness in this distant relative of the Grifo, the Bizzarrini 5300GT. But the car's construction was, however, completely different. It was built around a multi-tube frame rather than the pressed steel chassis of the Grifo.

This Mk III Cobra was certainly able to handle the 300–425bhp the 200lb (90kg) heavier 427 unit could push out in 'street' form, but the car was really a bit of a brute, with too much power for its own good. It also entered production too late for 1965 season race homologation, and after a rule change in international racing for 1966, Ford abandoned its support for the project. AC salvaged something by building a 289-engined Mk III until 1968, but there were few takers.

The new chassis was clearly too good to waste, so AC revised it to give a less firm ride and commissioned Italian stylist and coachbuilder Frua to produce a grand touring body for it. The result was the AC 428, first seen in 1965 and available until 1973 as either a convertible or a coupé. Around 70 of these hand-built gentleman's carriages were produced.

Carroll Shelby also had a hand in the development of the 1964 Sunbeam Tiger, a hastily conceived scissors-and-paste job that gave the tame Sunbeam Alpine sports car a Ford V8 transplant. The result was a crude but engaging hot rod that with its 260 engine (or 289 on the last cars) was the cheapest super-performance British sports machine on the market. However, the Tiger did not sell and was withdrawn in 1967 after a bare 7000 had been made.

Maserati at its peak

For those in search of a more refined and more European approach to high-performance motoring, Maserati with its finely engineered sixes and V8s was a company at its peak during this decade.

The 3500 series with its typical Maserati tubular chassis continued until 1964, as did the extravagant and bespoke 5000GT with its detuned V8 race engine. Then in 1963 two new and elegant models were introduced: the Frua-styled Mistral and, to replace the 3500GT, the Vignale-styled 2 + 2 Sebring. There was also a new eight, a four-door sedan called the Quattroporte: sober looking, but

stirringly powered by a 4135cc version of Maserati's quad-cam all-alloy V8. More sportingly inclined fans of the eight-cylinder Maserati had to wait until 1966, when the Mexico coupé was introduced.

Henceforth the V8 was, however, to be Maserati's favoured power plant, despite the fact that six-cylinder cars continued until 1970. And so in 1966 came the first of the new generation, the sharp-lined and broad-beamed Ghibli, a car far more flamboyant than Maserati's previous offerings. This was joined three years later by the nominally four-seater Indy, at first with the 4135cc V8, but latterly with the same 4.7-liter unit as the Ghibli.

These substantial coupés and convertibles were rather let down by their simple leaf-spring rear suspension. And when offered with power-assisted steering and automatic transmission they became more businessman's express than race-bred sports tourer: despite the delights of the smooth but potent four-cam V8 engine. Perhaps Maserati's withdrawal from competition in the 1960s was showing.

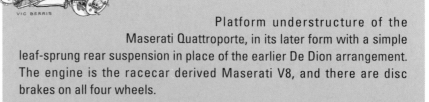

VIC BERRIS

Platform understructure of the Maserati Quattroporte, in its later form with a simple leaf-sprung rear suspension in place of the earlier De Dion arrangement. The engine is the racecar derived Maserati V8, and there are disc brakes on all four wheels.

Diversity at Maranello

No such accusation could be levelled at Ferrari, whose cars continued to be as hard-edged and charismatic as ever during the 1960s. Even leaving aside competition models such as the lovely GTO, Ferrari came up with some of the finest cars of the decade. The 250GT evolved in 1960 into the 250GTE 2 + 2 fastback, an elegant and well-received transformation that led in 1964 to the 4-liter slant-headlamp 330GT 2 + 2. More captivatingly, the short-wheelbase 250GT spawned the delectable Berlinetta Lusso of 1962, a superbly smooth, glassy Pininfarina shape that remains one of the finest bodies ever put on a Ferrari — and it was good for 140mph (225km/h) or more.

During the 1960s the 250 range and its descendants became the 'touring' side of the Ferrari range. The 330GT 2 + 2 gave way in 1967 to the altogether softer 365GT 2 + 2, with independent self-levelling rear suspension and power-assisted steering, and in 1971 this was displaced by the conservatively styled 365GT4, with a body shape that was to last for almost 20 years.

The more overtly sporting Ferrari models of the decade had their starting point in the aggressive 275GTB launched in 1964. For this high-waisted and long-snouted Pininfarina design the Ferrari

V12 was bored out to 3286cc, which meant 280bhp on six twin-choke Weber carburetors. More significantly, for the first time on a road Ferrari there was independent rear suspension, as well as a rear-mounted gearbox. Two years later came a new 300bhp quad-cam V12 with dry sump lubrication, directly evolved from the racing engines and giving improved torque and flexibility.

From the original twin-cam 275GTB was derived the 275GTS spider, using the same mechanicals but with slightly less power. Versions with 4-liter and 4.4-liter capacity followed, and were also available in coupé form as — respectively — the 330GTC and 365GTC. These mid-range models were probably some of the best all-round Ferraris of the 1960s, being taut, nimble and refined, with electrifying performance from the magnificent V12 engine.

In 1968 came the ultimate front-engined Ferrari: the legendary Daytona, or 365GTB/4. Drawing on the mechanical layout of the

A superb British grand tourer, the potent Chrysler-powered Jensen CV-8 was let down by its quirky styling.

This is the rear-drive Jensen Interceptor, identical to the FF but for the lack of the latter car's four-wheel drive and its Maxaret anti-lock brakes.

Nobody could accuse the new Jensen series introduced in 1966 of being ugly, and even today the Touring styling looks fresh. This is the innovative four-wheel-drive FF, recognizable by its twin side vents.

quad-cam 275GTB/4, its 4.4-liter V12 gave 352bhp, and maximum speed was an unbeatable 175mph (282km/h). This was the world's fastest car, yet it was a totally civilized and untemperamental touring coupé. When a current model it was described as an all-time great, and with the passing of the years that judgement still stands.

By the time of the Daytona, the big limited production Ferrari had finally faded out: after three series with a spectacularly graceful Pininfarina body called the *coupé aerodinamica*. Derived from a 1960 Turin show car, these machines culminated in the 500 Superfast of 1964–6. Big and beefy mechanically, and even a little crude with its cart-spring rear, the 500 Superfast had solid, assertive road behaviour with a no-compromise performance from its 400bhp 5-liter power unit. In its day it surely counted as the ultimate supercar.

Enter Lamborghini

Ferrari now had a new competitor, and a worthy one indeed: tractor and air conditioner manufacturer Ferruccio Lamborghini. Determined to produce a better car than a Ferrari — nothing fancy but just a totally effective and conventional grand tourer — Lamborghini brought together a team of talented young engineers and in 1963 announced his 350GTV model.

The new Lamborghini scored over Ferrari in having all-round independent suspension and a V12 with four camshafts instead of the Ferrari's twin cams, but its bodywork lacked elegance. All the same, the production 350GT did everything intended of it, and was a genuinely civilized high-performance car. The later Islero was more crisply styled, and was joined by the flashy four-seater Espada, but the real attention grabbing was done by an altogether different Lamborghini, of which more later.

Big-engined and brutish: the 7-liter 427 Cobra. Under the pumped-out skin is a new chassis with coil-spring independent suspension all round.

Aston Martin and Jaguar — Britain aims high

In Britain, Aston Martin was another manufacturer to go down the V8 route. This time, however, it was with an all-alloy engine of the company's own design, drawing on the splendid Aston twin-cam six for aspects of its layout. The resultant 5.3-liter unit used four cams and delivered around 338bhp. At last the DBS had the engine it had been designed for, and a 160mph (257km/h) maximum pushed the bulky four-seater firmly into the supercar class.

It is tempting to say that Jaguar was already there. That is not quite true, but with the E type it was certainly knocking on the door. At its launch in 1961 the E type created an absolute sensation. The looks had a lot to do with it: distilled out of the curvaceous Le Mans winning D type, the E type's lines were gloriously sensuous and exuded power.

But under that taut feline skin was engineering to match:

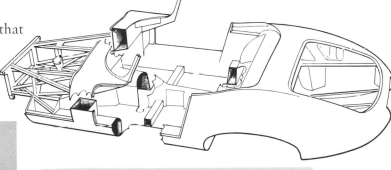

Heart of the Jaguar E type. Despite myth, the structure is relatively simple, and comprises a not especially complex monocoque 'tub' to which a square-tube subframe is bolted to carry the engine and the front suspension. Reproduction bodies are now available.

Gentleman's hotrod: Cobra mechanicals plus Frua body equals AC 428. This desirable equation was available to the discerning from 1965 until 1973.

Hydrolastic suspension was introduced in the Austin/Morris. The tail rises in response to upward motion of front wheels eliminating pitch.

The nose rises in response to upward motion of rear wheels, again eliminating pitch.

Suspension stiffens in response to upward motion of front and rear wheels, giving controlled, level, vertical movement.

independent rear suspension, four-wheel disc brakes (inboard at the rear), and — of course — that superb XK twin-cam engine. All this, furthermore, was wrapped in an advanced monocoque structure with a spaceframe front end to carry the front suspension and the engine.

Never mind that the test car which reached 150mph (241km/h) was definitely non-standard: here was a British model that did everything the Continental glamour cars did, and generally did it better, all for a fraction of the price. The E type immediately became the hottest international automotive property, and one of the most instantly recognizable shapes in the world. For once, worth fully matched image.

A tame Mercedes, a revived BMW

Jaguar's 1950s competition rival, Mercedes, stepped back from the high-performance market with the 1963 launch of its 230SL sports car. Using a fuel-injected version of its 2.3-liter overhead-cam six, the German car was in fact more of a grand-touring convertible than an out-and-out sports machine. With power steering and an auto gearbox as options, enthusiasts were not quite sure what to make of the 230SL. However, its performance was reasonable enough, it handled and rode well, and was of undoubted quality. It also won friends for its delicate styling and attractive 'pagoda roof' hardtop. Maybe it was just too mature a car for the average sports car owner?

Evolving into bigger-engined 250SL and 280SL models, the series was current until 1971, and laid down design parameters that can still be seen in today's third generation SL.

Meanwhile, Mercedes' high-quality rival BMW had started to pull itself round with its lightweight sporting sedans, starting with the 1500 of 1961. This led to the delightful little 1600 two-door and its more potent 2002 sister, and ultimately to a new six-cylinder BMW. These two strands, the four- and the six-cylinders, were

Don Pither, well-known in historic rallying, exercises his ex-works Sunbeam Tiger: a beefed-up Sunbeam Alpine with a 4.2-liter Ford V8. Later cars had the 4.7-liter 289 unit. Unlike the Alpine, the Tiger has rack-and-pinion steering.

brought together in 1968 to create one of the finer sporting coupés of the late 1960s: the 2800CS.

All that was involved was to insert the new 170bhp ohc six into the elegant coupé body created by Karmann for the 2000 sedan floorpan. The result was a sweet-natured and well-apppointed car with refinement to match its looks. More importantly, it provided an excellent basis for BMW's participation in the European Touring Car race championship, and led to the all-conquering lightweight CSL models of the 1970s.

Open-air fun

But what of the British sports car? It was alive and well during the 1960s, with ever-improving Austin-Healeys and Triumph TRs, a new monocoque MG, and a standard-setting Lotus.

The Elite had not been a success, so for the Elan of 1962 Lotus played safe, and used a simple folded-steel backbone chassis under the predictable fiberglass bodyshell. It also discarded the rough and expensive Coventry-Climax engine of the Elite in favour of its own twin-cam conversion of Ford's new Anglia engine. This endowed the 1484lb (673kg) Lotus with a

superb power-to-weight ratio and, along with the Elan's phenomenal roadholding and handling — without the penalty of a harsh ride — made the car a true giant-killer. 'If the E type is king, we continue to regard the Elan as prince,' wrote *Motor* magazine, who dubbed the diminutive Lotus 'one of the finest sports cars in the world'.

For those who could not afford the Lotus or who, not without reason, mistrusted its kit-car fragility, there was the safe option of the MGB, a soundly engineered 1.8-liter that had no real vices and a great many virtues. It is fashionable to sneer at the MGB, but its conventional mechanicals delivered the goods and were capable of easy modification for higher performance. The tragedy of the MG was that seemingly pigheaded management in the parent company failed to invest in the car's development, so it eventually became an embarrassing antique. Nonetheless, the MGB remains one of the best all-round sports cars of the post-Second World War years.

Certainly an antique, but by no means an embarrassing one, was the Morgan. In its essentials unchanged since 1936, it became one of the most exciting sports cars of the 1960s when in 1968 it received the lightweight ex-Buick Rover V8. The ride was still unyielding, limiting roadholding on all but the smoothest surfaces, and the ash-framed body soon shook or rotted itself to bits, but the 3½-liter V8 gave the primitive but endearing Plus Eight a devastating performance. Few motoring experiences are as invigorating, for those with sufficient stamina.

Golden years for the Corvette

Brute power of an altogether more unsubtle nature came from the Chevrolet Corvette, for which the 1960s were without a doubt the golden years. The 'Vette entered the decade with power increases continuing year on year, such that in 1961 the injected 'fuelie' 283

Cutaways show construction of Lotus Elan (above) and Lotus Europa (right). Both are bodied in fiberglass and both use a simple folded-steel backbone chassis. Note the 'Chapman strut' rear suspension on the Elan, and the mid-mounted Renault 16 engine of the Europa.

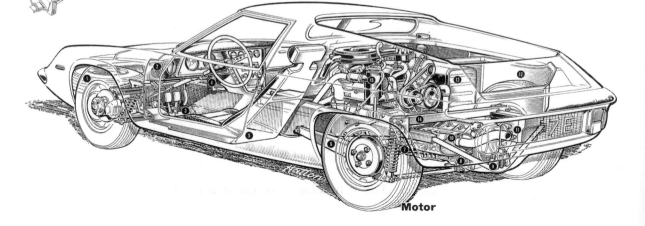

A restrained and beautifully honed development of conservative high-class British engineering: the Alvis TE. These cars had bodies by Mulliner Park Ward, based on a style created by Swiss coachbuilder Graber. They used a straightforward in-line 3-liter six in a conventional chassis with a coil-and-wishbone front end and a semi-elliptic rear.

pushed out 315bhp and delivered a 0–60mph (0–100km/h) time of a blistering 5.5 seconds. The real action, however, came with the 1963 model year, when the first all-new Corvette since the car's 1953 launch hit the showrooms.

Shorter, lighter, stronger and more stylish, the 1963 Corvette Sting Ray had a new ladder frame with independent rear suspension — for the first time on a modern American-made car. It also had a stunning body by the GM styling chief Bill Mitchell, featuring concealed headlamps, powerful moulding lines and, most controversially, a split rear window on the coupé. 'If you take that off, you might as well forget the whole thing,' said Mitchell.

The Sting Ray did not just look good, it also delivered performance to match — by the truckload. The 'small block' V8s were potent enough, but for 1965 a 'big block' 6½-liter engine was introduced, delivering 425bhp. The following year came a 7-liter 427, which in limited-run 1967 L-88 form put out 560bhp. This was

overkill for all but incurable horsepower junkies, and the 'small block' Corvettes are decidely more agreeable and practical than the obscenely over-endowed 'big block' cars.

The 'Vette was restyled for 1968, but ended up heavier, less spacious, less well-constructed, and more gimmick-laden. Things came right after some careful development, but the long-lived cars of 1968–83 never had the charisma of their immediate predecessors.

The first Maserati 5000GT was built for the Shah of Iran, and the clientele for the remaining 32 cars was similarly elevated. The outrageously expensive 5000 used a little-changed version of Maserati's sports-racing V8 engine. The car in the foreground is bodied by Frua, that at the rear by Allemano.

'Put it in the middle'

The Chevrolet must have seemed like just so much ironmongery to the Italians, who with the Lamborghini Miura were taking the next big leap forward in supercar design. Inspired by the example of Ferrari and Ford sports-racers, Lamborghini was the first manufacturer of note to espouse the mid-engine configuration. Shown first as a rolling chassis in 1965, the Miura used the Lamborghini V12 mounted transversely behind the driver, in a sheet-steel punt frame. The following year these tantalizing mechanicals were clothed in one of the most dramatic bodies ever to be produced by an Italian styling house.

Bertone's creation was lean, low and tautly drawn over the seductive mechanicals underneath. It was easy to think that such an artistic delight could never live up to its too good to be true looks, but the Miura was every bit the equal of its styling. It had well-balanced handling, impressive high-speed stability (despite a lack of spoilers), and an acceptably comfortable ride: not to mention a top speed of over 170mph (274km/h). Heavy controls and high noise levels were a small price to pay for such a package.

Ferrari joined the mid-engined club a little later, and at a different level, with its delightful Dino, which finally entered production in 1969. Powered by a Fiat-manufactured Ferrari V6 intended for Formula 2 racing, it again had the engine mounted transversely, and started out as a two-liter, called the 206GT. It was rapidly given a bigger 2418cc power unit, however, and renamed the 246GT. The new engine had a cast-iron block in place of the alloy block used on the original Dino, and the bodywork was

GREAT CARS OF THE WORLD

now in steel rather than the aluminium of the 206.

The quad-cam V6 was a true Ferrari unit, invigoratingly alive at all times, and the chassis had the superb poise you would expect. Later Dinos, bigger and V8-powered, never quite captured the essential 'rightness' of the first of the breed.

Porsche introduces a legend

In Germany, 1963 brought a new Porsche: a modest little coupé powered by a new flat-six air-cooled 2-liter delivering 130bhp. The engine featured a single overhead cam per bank, dry-sump lubrication, and a very stiff crankshaft. It was mounted behind the rear axle, Beetle-style, but there was now semi-trailing rear suspension in place of the 356's simple swing-axles. Called the 911 when it entered production in 1964, the new Porsche clearly had a promising specification; but could anyone have ever predicted the extent to which the 911 would exceed that promise?

Here is not the place to detail the staggering competition history of the 911 and its derivatives. Just as impressive, however, is the way the road car evolved. Initially a fast but not over-fast tourer blessed with skittish handling, the 911 became available as a 160bhp 911S in 1966; by 1970 the engine was a 2341cc unit putting out 190bhp, with much improved torque. The chassis had also by then been carefully honed, so that in sensible hands it maintained a slight degree of understeer. However, imprudent driving, particularly on wet roads, would provoke the old Porsche bogy of oversteer that was difficult to catch — but at much higher speeds than was originally the case. Development would continue apace in the following decade.

Two generations of Maserati Quattroporte: the original 5000-derived car of 1963–71 and the Quattroporte III of 1976–8. In between there was a short-lived Quattroporte II built around the Citroën SM floorpan and mechanicals.

Mistrale in coupé form is again Frua styled.

Advances for everyman

The 1960s were just as important a time for more ordinary cars. Indeed it was a period that saw some of the greatest four-door sedans of the postwar era. Some are so commonplace today that it takes a historian's perspective to accord them their due; others have had adulation heaped on them from the moment of their introduction.

In the first category falls the BMC 1100, best known as an Austin or a Morris but sold under several other names. Created by Mini designer Alec Issigonis, it was the most advanced small sedan in the world when it was announced in 1962. Featuring the same space-efficient transverse engine and front-wheel drive as the Mini, it added to this an interconnected rubber-and-fluid suspension that was unique at the time and gave a comfortable and controlled ride, with Mini standards of roadholding.

With pleasing Pininfarina styling, the compact 1100 made its rear-engined competitors from continental Europe look seriously obsolete. Unfortunately, poor quality and inept marketing and after sales support, meant that the 1100's success was limited to Britain — where it dominated the market for many years.

Another currently unsung design is the Renault 16, a front-wheel-drive 1½-liter that in 1965 pioneered the modern hatchback format. With its versatile interior and typically French soft ride, it was a refined and practical mid-class car.

More readily recognized as a great design, at least in Britain, is the Rover 2000 series introduced in 1963. Creatively engineered in the Rover manner, it was built around a base unit (giving easy accident repairs and a deformable safety cage);

Maserati Indy, sister car to the two-seater Ghibli coupé.

had a de Dion rear axle — to reduce unsprung weight and to keep the rear wheels always parallel to each other; and pioneered the compact 'executive' car. Combining thoughtful design and quality assembly, the Rover had a dynamic competence comfortably above that of its more orthodox rivals.

Orthodoxy was certainly not something of which the striking wedge-shaped NSU Ro80 could be accused. For a small independent company better known for its motorcycles the 1967 Ro80 was an extraordinary achievement. Not only was this German car the world's first rotary-engined sedan: it was also the most daringly efficient in its aerodynamics, had a front-wheel-drive chassis that even today feels modern, and topped it all off with a fascinating semi-automatic transmission. The NSU was beguilingly refined, with that ultra-smooth Wankel rotary, and it was one of the biggest automotive tragedies of the time that its brave engine was blighted by poor durability.

Jaguar's XJ6 of 1968 was altogether more conservative, being a considered evolution of previous Jaguar practice. This evolution centred on painstaking development of Jaguar's all-independent suspension, with particular attention being paid to bushing and to effective anti-dive geometry. The result was a car offering Rolls-Royce refinement, Jaguar performance, and sports car roadholding. Admittedly the XK engine was a bit long in the tooth, but it was a fine unit, and the superlative V12 was just around the corner.

Clever, considered British engineering at its best: the Rover P6 2000. Clearly shown here is the De Dion rear axle with inboard disc brakes. The unusual horizontal position for the front springs was intended to allow room for a gas-turbine engine.

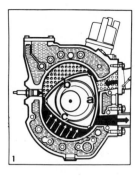
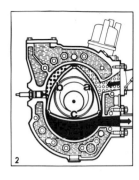
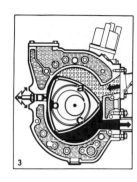
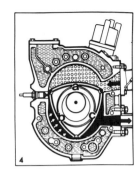

How the Wankel engine works: the four strokes of the engine — induction, compression, expansion, exhaust — occur exactly as in a normal reciprocating engine, but in an even flow of rotary motion. When the triangular piston has rotated once, it has completed the four-stroke cycle three times.

Ferrari's famed Gran Turismo Omologato, or GTO: a homologation special built between 1961 and 1964. It was intended to rival the Aston Martin DB4GT Zagato and the lightweight Jaguar E type in the GT championship, which was new for 1962. It was lighter, more powerful and better aerodynamically than the preceding 250GT Berlinetta. The styling was by Ferrari, not by Pininfarina.

A touring Ferrari with almost the cachet of the racing GTO: the 250GT Berlinetta Lusso, one of Pininfarina's most eye-catching shapes for the Maranello marque.

The 330GT 2 + 2 was the first big-engined Ferrari to be made in substantial numbers — around 1100 were produced. The engine was a 3967cc unit.

The 275GTB quad cam. This four-cam dry-sump power unit pushed out 300bhp. The engine and the transaxle transmission were features carried over to the subsequent Ferrari Daytona.

Last of the big old-fashioned Ferrari models, the stunning 500 Superfast of 1964–6. The shape derives from a 1960 Turin show car. In its day this was the ultimate Ferrari.

The Daytona, Ferrari's front-engined late-1960s supercar. A convertible version was also offered, but only 125 or so were built, out of a total run of 1400 Daytonas. This coupé has the headlamps behind flaps. Later examples had them behind a transparent plastic cowl.

The Lamborghini 3464cc all-alloy V12 delivered 336bhp for the 350GT, and in 3929cc 400GT form put out 360bhp. It was a quad-cam unit.

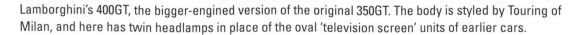

Lamborghini's 400GT, the bigger-engined version of the original 350GT. The body is styled by Touring of Milan, and here has twin headlamps in place of the oval 'television screen' units of earlier cars.

The Aston Martin
DB4GT Zagato was an
attempt to produce a
rival to the Ferrari GTO.
Mechanically it was
the same as the
ordinary DB4GT apart
from a raised
compression ratio.
However, these cars
proved unable to best
the Ferraris, and
demanded rather more
from their drivers.

Ultimate evolution of the series initiated by the
DB4: the Aston Martin DB6. Instantly
recognizable by its squared-off tail with spoiler,
the DB6 also had a longer wheelbase.

Wonderful sculpture: the triple-SU XK engine
of the Jaguar 3.8 E type.

The Jaguar E type was introduced in 1961 in both open and closed
fastback coupé forms - the ungainly 2 + 2 coupé only arrived in 1966.
Here a 3.8-liter coupé poses with a Chevrolet Corvette.

Classic shape: the open E type, again in 3.8-liter
form. The 4.2-liter engine came in 1964
and offered stronger bottom-end torque.

The lightweight E type had an aluminium monocoque and alloy panels, along with an aluminium engine block. This resulted in a car around 500lb (227kg) lighter than the normal E type. This is one of three cars entered by Briggs Cunningham in the 1963 Le Mans 24 Hours.

Heavy metal: Jaguar's replacement for the Mk IX was the Mk X of 1961, with monocoque construction and independent rear suspension. The chrome side strip identifies this as the last version, the 420G.

Fast, well-appointed and good-looking, the Mk 2 Jaguar sedans were highly popular. The more substantial bumpers identify the front car as an earlier model than the white example behind; wire wheels were optional. There was also a Daimler version of the Mk 2, using the Daimler 2½-liter V8 first seen in the SP250 sports car.

Beautifully executed interiors have always been a feature of Jaguars. This is a 3.8-liter Mk 2.

The new Mercedes 230SL sports car of 1963 was a tame beast after the 300SL, although a move up on the 300SL's lesser sibling, the heavy 190SL. The new model was progressively up-engined, becoming a 250SL in 1967 and a 280SL a year later. Physically these cars are identical.

One of the most sought-after postwar BMWs, the elegant six-cylinder CS coupé. Introduced in 1965 as the four-cylinder 2000C and 2000CS, the Karmann body received the engine it so deserved in 1968, to become the 2800CS. This is a later 3.0CS model.

The Lotus Elan in its final Sprint form. With its light weight, superb roadholding, and handling, and powerful twin-cam engine the little Elan set the dynamic standard for 1960s sports cars.

The Elan's engine was a twin-cam conversion of the Ford Kent engine used in Cortinas and the like. Capacity was 1558cc, and power in its big-valve Sprint form was 126bhp.

The most extraordinary sports car of the 1960s, the Lotus Europa was originally intended as a hi-tech replacement for the Lotus Seven. It featured a mid-mounted Renault 16 engine and the most aerodynamically efficient body on a production car. In its first form it also had countless impractical cost-cutting measures. This is a later S2 version, in the company of a rear-engined Alpine-Renault.

In 1971 the Europa was given the Lotus twin-cam engine. The appreciably improved car also had the flying buttresses at the rear cut down to improve visibility. Roadholding and handling remained phenomenal.

MG's new unitary construction sports car of 1962, the MGB, lasted until 1980 and was also available from 1965 in fastback GT form. So great a following does the 'B' have that production of the monocoque shell has been restarted, and a short run of updated MGBs is being manufactured by the parent company, the Rover Group.

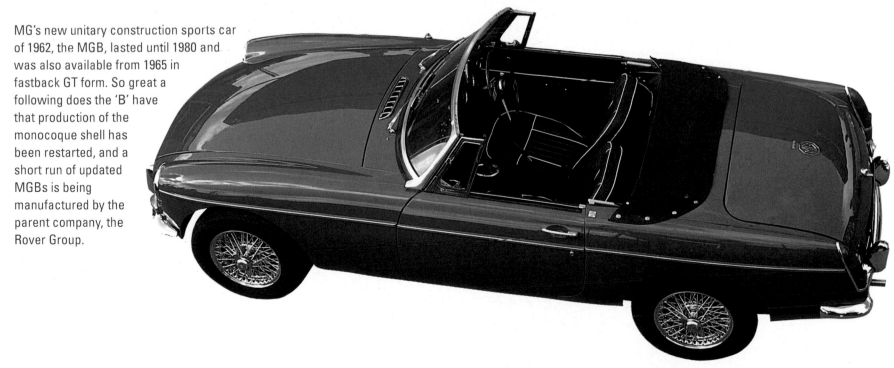

John Cooper himself at the wheel of a Mk I Mini-Cooper: not a higher-powered Cooper S but the plain Cooper with either a 997cc or 998cc twin-carb version of the A series engine. The Mini-Coopers, and more particularly the Cooper S, were serious rivals to the traditional British sports car.

Morgan's antiquated Plus Four was transformed when in 1968 it was given the ex-Buick Rover V8 in place of its Triumph TR 'big four'. The new car, called the Plus Eight, is still very much in production, and in its current 3.9-liter injected form has electrifying performance.

A Japanese cat among the British pigeons? Honda's S800 boasted a howling all-alloy 791cc engine with twin overhead cam four carburetors, and roller-bearing crank. Behind are a Triumph Spitfire Mk III and an Austin-Healey Sprite Mk IV.

The Honda S800 engine draws on motorcycle practice. The bodies to the Keihin carburetors are cast in pairs, but the carbs are in effect like four SU-type units.

Honda's little 791cc buzz-bomb, the S800. Built on a separate box section chassis, its engineering is seemingly nothing out of the ordinary, until you look at the engine. Earlier variants had drive taken from the differential to the rear wheels by chain.

In 1969 there arrived a new Japanese contender for the American sports car market: the Datsun 240Z, a simply engineered 2.4-liter straight-six with independent rear suspension. It was a great success, unlike the six-cylinder MGC in the background of this shot.

The Chevrolet Corvette reached its peak with the 1963–7 cars, independently suspended at the rear and with a striking new body by GM design chief Bill Mitchell. This is a 1966 roadster with the big block 427 engine.

Split-window coupé: this feature is only found on the first year's Corvettes.

The next generation 'Vette introduced for the 1968 model year was regarded as something of a disappointment at the time. This is an LT-1, with the high-performance small block engine introduced in 370bhp form for 1970.

Lamborghini stunned the motoring world when the company introduced the Miura in 1966. The transversely set V12 initially developed 350bhp, but in the Miura's final 1971-2 SV form output was up to 385bhp.

The de Tomaso Mangusta: somewhat uncivilized, with a mid-mounted Ford V8 that gave the car wayward handling, but with the compensation of a dramatic body with gullwing engine covers.

The Dino 246GT: one of the finest Ferrari models of all time, although technically speaking it was a Dino and not a Ferrari, because it did not have a 12-cylinder engine.

A fascinating hybrid: the Fiat Dino, with Ferrari Dino engine. The open cars are by Pininfarina, the coupés by Bertone. At first the engine was a 2-liter but this was uprated to 2.4 liters in 1969, when the leaf-spring rear was replaced by a coil-spring independent set-up.

The BMC 1100 was the world's most advanced small sedan when introduced in 1962, and for many years it topped the British bestsellers list. This is an early Morris version.

Last of the Porsche 356 line, the 356C of 1964-5. Disc brakes were the main innovation and engines were all 1600s, in three stages of tune.

The evergreen Porsche 911 in its original small-bumper form. The car in the main shot is actually quite a rarity, a 2-liter in 140bhp tune with the two-pedal Sportomatic transmission.

Renault's pioneering
family hatchback,
the 16, with supple
torsion-bar suspension
and a versatile seating
configuration.

The Alfa Romeo Giulia berlina
may look odd to some eyes, but
its shape is aerodynamically
surprisingly efficient. Alfa's twin-
cam engine, a five-speed gearbox,
and a well-controlled coil-sprung
live axle add up to a pleasant
sporting package.

A fine example of the 'Chinese Eye' Rolls-Royce, a Silver Cloud III with coachwork by Mulliner Park Ward to a design by Graber of Switzerland. The shape dates to 1957, but the slanting twin headlamps only came in during 1963.

Mercedes aimed at the Rolls-Royce market with its 600 model, introduced in 1963. It was available in some extraordinary long-wheelbase forms, but this is the regular version with only four doors and a more manageable length of platform.

GREAT CARS OF THE WORLD

Daimler's Majestic Major was an unsung hero of the 1960s luxury car scene: an apparently staid sedan packing a 4½-liter V8 and blessed with impressive road behaviour.

Rover's 2000 series, known as the P6, was a testament to the creative engineering of the Rover company during the post-Second World War years. It had a safety cage base-unit construction, an interior with four bucket seats and, in 2000 and later 2200 form, an alloy-head ohc four-cylinder engine.

Still looking fresh after all these years, the 1967 NSU Ro80. Aerodynamically efficient, with a well-honed chassis and a spacious and airy interior, the front-drive NSU was let down by the unreliability of its most advanced feature of all, its twin-rotor Wankel engine.

The finest possible testament to Sir William Lyons and his team:
the superb Jaguar XJ6 of 1968. This is one of the original series,
with the low-set front bumper.

6

Riding the Storm

The 1970s began with a crazy exuberance, typified by such cars as the hydropneumatically sprung Citroën SM and the outlandish Lamborghini Countach — not to mention perhaps the most bizarre role change for years, the transformation of Bertone's Stratos styling exercise into the all-conquering Lancia Stratos rally car.

The SM: Citroën does it again

The SM was an extraordinary technological achievement, and at the time of its 1970 launch was the most complex car ever to have reached production. Powered by an all-alloy quad-cam Maserati V6 of 2670cc, it added a further refinement to the DS-derived hydropneumatic system: VariPower variable assistance steering powered to self-centre automatically. Then there was the sculptural body, like that of no other car before or since, and with a drag coefficient of only 0.25.

Intimidating in town, the bulky SM was a car for the open roads and for effortless magic carpet grand touring, revelling in that wonderful self-levelling suspension, instantly responsive steering and torquey V6 engine. Regrettably, the fuel crisis and the Peugeot takeover of Citroën caused production to be stopped in 1975, after fewer than 13,000 of these magnificent but demanding cars had been built.

In compensation, Citroën's other new model of 1970, the medium-sized flat-four GS, soon established itself as one of the benchmark cars in its class, thanks to its hydropneumatic suspension and clean, aerodynamically efficient styling.

The GS was not alone, however, for it was rivalled by

Citroën's astounding SM, with a Maserati V6 driving the front wheels. Power output of the 170bhp engine was raised by 8bhp with the introduction of fuel-injection in 1972 and a year later a 3-liter automatic version was announced. The two inner lamps on each side turn with the steering.

An unexpected rival to the Citroën GS came from Alfa Romeo, who in 1971 introduced the Alfasud. Initially an extremely cheap popular sedan, with fit and finish to match, it gradually moved up market from its original 1186cc form but always retained its superb road manners.

another classic 1970s sedan, the Alfasud. Nearly identical in size to the Citroën, the front-wheel-drive Alfasud had a crisp water-cooled flat-four power unit and a beautifully sorted chassis that gave it the best handling and roadholding in its class. Unfortunately, however, standards of construction and of rustproofing were diabolical.

The ultimate supercars: Countach and Boxer

Compared with these humble family cars the Lamborghini Countach seemed to belong to another planet. First seen at the 1971 Geneva motor show as a Bertone concept car, it entered production in 1974 as a no-expense-spared replacement for the Miura.

The mid-engined Countach used the Lamborghini V12 mounted longitudinally, with the gearbox projecting forward, and was built around a multi-tube frame to which ultra-thin aluminium panelling was fixed. Running gear was to competition standards of design and construction, with much use of magnesium alloy castings.

It was the flamboyant body, however, with its swing-up doors, aggressive air scoops and recessed NACA ducts, that made the Countach such an object of automotive lust. Investigate beyond the pin-up looks, however, and there was performance and road manners to match: a 180mph (290km/h) maximum speed, with flat cornering, well-balanced handling, and a supple ride. Those who pronounced the Countach 'the ultimate road car' were not indulging in hollow sensationalism: it was true.

Ferrari's counterpart, the 365GT/4 Berlinetta Boxer, was first seen in 1971 and seemed almost dowdy by comparison. It gave nothing away, however, to the flashy Lamborghini. Capable of 171mph (275km/h), the 4.4-liter Boxer was another mid-engined design, where for more efficient space utilization the gearbox was placed underneath the engine. To make this possible, the traditional Ferrari V12 was discarded in favour of a flat-12 (or 'boxer') derived from Ferrari's similar racing car power units. In the same way the chassis drew on competition practice, and was based on tubular structure panelled in steel. Both more sporting and more practical than the Lamborghini, the Boxer came across less as a fashion accessory and more as a car for the user-enthusiast.

The breathtaking Lamborghini Countach's film star looks hide racing standard running gear and a gearbox-forward, longitudinally mounted V12. Initially this was of 3929cc, but the car in our photo is a 1985 four-valve-per cylinder *quattrovalvole* with a 5.2-liter power unit developing 455bhp. *Autocar* magazine clocked it at 178mph (286km/h).

The second division

A notch below the Boxer and Countach in the supercar stakes was Maserati's mid-engined Bora. Heavier than either, the Bora was powered by the Maserati V8 in 4.7-liter form and was good for over 160mph (257km/h). In character less overtly sporting than some of its mid-engined rivals, it was a splendid grand tourer with muscular performance and massive reserves of roadholding. There was a little sister, too, the V6-powered 2+2 Merak, which used a simplified version of the Bora's Giugiaro-styled body.

Rather less subtle than the finely engineered Maseratis was the De Tomaso Pantera, a 1970 follow-up to the striking but supposedly evil-handling backbone-chassis Mangusta. Produced with Ford backing as a cut-price supercar to be sold in substantial numbers through American Lincoln-Mercury dealers, the Pantera promised much and delivered a fair amount, but was ultimately let down by imperfect design and execution.

Ford soon pulled out, but the Pantera, powered by a meaty Ford V8, has continued through into the 1990s. Made in small numbers, latterly with preposterous body add-ons, it has always offered exciting but flawed supercar motoring.

The 1970s were the years when the mid-engined layout was most in vogue, and a period when Ferrari and Lamborghini locked horns with rival V8-powered junior supercars, both styled by Bertone. The Lamborghini Uracco and its later Silhouette and Jalpa derivatives eventually fizzled out, but the Ferrari 308 GT4 led to a successful breed of more elegant Pininfarina-styled cars that lasted to the end of the 1980s. Although lacking the delightful litheness of the Dino 246, the 308 GTB and its targa-topped GTS derivative were invigorating restatements of the Ferrari ethos and the V8 car,

The Ferrari 365GT/4 Berlinetta Boxer began life in 1971 with a 4.4-liter flat-12, but was up-engined to 4.9 liters in 1976 to become the 512BB. Four triple-choke Weber carburetors were retained until 1981, when fuel injection was introduced. Here a 512 poses with the car the Boxer replaced, the legendary Daytona.

A dose of reality

The 1970s were not, however, a supercar-studded dream decade: far from it. The fuel crisis of 1973–4 brought the high flyers to earth with a bang. The American muscle car was already dead by then, smothered by clean air regulations; the small European specialist marques fell next.

Jensen and Iso went to the wall, and Maserati and Aston Martin changed hands after a time when their future looked grim. The heady days of the 7-liter stormers suddenly seemed ancient history, a message Ford seemed to drive home when it brought out a new Mustang with a puny 2.3-liter four-cylinder unit.

once marginalized as a Dino, soon became the mainstay of the Maranello range.

The Lancia Stratos was a breed apart from these well-groomed grand tourers. Prompted by a 1970 Bertone styling exercise, the Stratos was the first of the purpose-built 'homologation-special' rally cars. Yet on its 1971 appearance it seemed nothing more than a fanciful Bertone ideas car.

From the start, however, the car was envisaged as a limited-production rally car, and under its abrupt wedge-shaped bodywork was a transversely mounted Ferrari Dino V6 sitting in a strong steel hull. This dramatic confection worked, and pulled in 82 international rally wins between 1972 and 1979. Super-fast and with go-kart responses, the Stratos redefined the rally car - although it took a brave man to tame the oversteering tendencies of the short-wheelbase Lancia.

In such a climate, Lotus appeared to be the torchbearer for a new motoring morality when it moved upmarket in 1974 and launched its efficient, high-performing, environmentally clean two-liter Elite. Building on the Elan configuration of a backbone chassis and fiberglass body, the Elite featured an ingenious shell moulded in two parts and joined at the waist. Power came from the 1973cc all-alloy slant-four first seen in ill-

The Ferrari V8 was first seen in the 308 GT4 of 1973–80, and has become the Maranello firm's principal power unit. It is a quad-cam all-alloy unit, and in the later form shown here it has four valves per cylinder and a capacity of 3185cc.

Maserati's Bora had elements of Citroën technology, as a result of the French firm taking over Maserati in 1968. Not only the brakes but also the seats were actuated by pressurised Citroën hydraulics. The body styling is by Giugiaro.

developed form in the Jensen-Healey sports car of 1972.

The Elite's quality was uncertain for some years, and the engine really only came right in its later 2.2-liter form, but the lightweight Lotus was a predictably clever design that showed that a high-performance car did not have to be flashy and multi-cylindered. The subsequent fastback Eclat version was developed into the highly regarded Excel, and this has only recently ceased production.

Lotus's ambitions did not stop with the Elite: in 1975 it announced a new mid-engined model to take over from the Europa. The Esprit used the same engine as the Elite, mounted longitudinally in a traditional Lotus backbone chassis. With a Giugiaro-styled wedge-shaped body, the Esprit was a striking car aimed squarely at those who coveted the likes of a Porsche, Ferrari or Maserati. In finish and detailing the Lotus still betrayed its humble parentage, but by the same token its superb chassis behaviour reflected its race-bred heritage.

Another British manufacturer to join the 'folded paper' school of sharp-edged styling was Aston Martin, whose new owners revived the Lagonda marque for a wedge-shaped four-door sedan based around DBS V8 mechanicals. First seen in 1976 but only entering production in 1978, the Lagonda appeared extraordinarily futuristic. This was not just because of the shape: in addition the interior featured electronic gas plasma and digital instrumentation, and touch-sensitive switchgear. As an eye-catching and long-legged luxury sedan it was unrivalled, and it provided an interesting counterpoint to the 'Bulldog British' Aston Martin coupés. These, incidentally, received quite a bit of development during the 1970s, for a brutal-looking 370bhp Vantage version was introduced in 1977 and a convertible Volante the following year.

Turbos, tourers and twelves

By this stage of the 1970s optimism was returning, and with it cars such as the Porsche 911 Turbo, a potent statement of that company's technological prowess, honed by race track success. Following on from the stripped-out 2.7-liter Carrera and its 3-liter successor, the Carrera RS 3.0, the Turbo was instantly recognizable

One of the 'forgotten Ferraris', this is a 365GTC/4, only made in 1971 and 1972. The 4.4-liter four-cam engine is a slightly detuned wet-sump version of the Daytona unit. The gearbox is mounted in unit with the engine rather than Daytona-style at the rear.

subcontracted development and production to Lamborghini: the Italian firm was in grave difficulties at the time, and ended up in receivership. Consequently the plans to compete in Group 5 went by the board. Instead a special M1 championship was devised, and lasted two seasons; this enabled a total of 399 roadgoing M1s to be built, along with 50 racers.

Current between 1978 and 1981, the M1 used BMW's classic straight-six, only with a twin-cam alloy head with four valves per cylinder. Its capacity was 3423cc, and power output was 280bhp for the road cars, 470bhp for racing, and around 850bhp in turbocharged Group 5 trim. This power unit was fitted in a tubular spaceframe clothed with a fiberglass body styled by Giugiaro's Ital Design.

The result was a businesslike coupé with a surprisingly tractable engine, staggeringly high cornering powers, and a 162mph (260km/h) maximum speed. For a detuned racing car the M1 was astonishingly civilized. It was essentially peripheral to BMW's main concerns, however, so its short life came as no shock.

Meanwhile, Porsche had stunned industry watchers by coming up with the pudgy, front-engined 928, a V8-powered grand tourer that was a breed apart from the taut rear-engined 911. Introduced in 1977, it seemed to make sense at the time: a mature, civilized and maybe even a little lazy 2 + 2, perfect for covering long distances in relaxed comfort but still with Porsche standards of performance, handling and roadholding.

However, the all-alloy 4474cc V8 delivered only 240bhp, giving performance inferior to that of a 911 Carrera; but then the 928 was less of a sports car. But when it also proved to have less refinement than its grand touring competitors, the critics became confused: what sort of car was the Porsche 928 trying to be ?

by its 'picnic tray' rear spoiler and aggressively flared arches. It screamed 'power' just standing still, and a 2994cc turbocharged engine fulfilled the promise of these looks by punching out 260bhp and 254lbft (345Nm) of torque. In 1977 there was an increase in capacity to 3299cc, boosting power to 300bhp.

The Turbo was no raw pseudo-racer, for it was impressively docile despite its rocketship performance, which was matched by phenomenal levels of grip. It was, said the critics, the only truly practical supercar. The Porsche 911 had come an awful long way in its 11 years of life...

Powerful cars were acceptable again, and even conservative BMW felt moved to create another German supercar, the mid-engined M1. The idea was to make what was essentially a competition model, to field against Porsche in Group 5 racing. Unfortunately the project went rather wrong when BMW

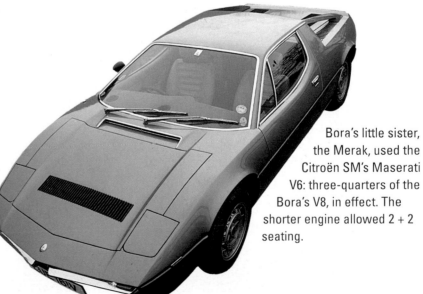

Bora's little sister, the Merak, used the Citroën SM's Maserati V6: three-quarters of the Bora's V8, in effect. The shorter engine allowed 2 + 2 seating.

Since those early days the 928 has been given progressively more power, and has been endowed with a more sporting edge. Nevertheless traditional Porsche drivers have preferred to stick with the 911. Sales have now dropped right away: which is a shame, as the 928 has evolved into what is probably the finest sporting grand tourer on the market. Maybe such a hybrid beast was always too much of a contradiction to be successful.

In going over to eight cylinders Porsche was a move behind Jaguar, who in 1971 had taken the bold step of introducing the world's first mass-production V12. Initially it was fitted to the British company's E type, aged by then, an installation that emphasized that car's degeneration into a softly suspended *boulevardier*. For the new 5.3-liter V12 was no sports car engine: it was a lazy, mildly tuned power unit giving seductive smoothness, silence and flexibility. It was gorgeous but its proper place was really in cars such as the XJ-S and XJ12.

With the new engine, the Jaguar XJ sedan became more than ever the most competent in the world, albeit at the expense of somewhat poor fuel consumption. At last the superbly developed chassis of the XJ6 had a power unit fully worthy of it, and the XJ12 embarrassed even the Rolls-Royce Silver Shadow, so high were its levels of refinement.

De Tomaso's replacement for the Mangusta, the Pantera. This is a 1972 model with various non-original features. During its early years the Pantera proved to have numerous structural and mechanical problems. This caused Ford-US to abandon collaborating with De Tomaso on the car.

For many years the only quantity production modern 12 cylinder engine was Jaguar's superb 5.3 liter V12. It is of all alloy construction, with a single cam per bank. Power in its original form was 272bhp at 5850rpm.

Utility with class

A technical achievement of an altogether different kind was the four-wheel-drive Range-Rover of 1970. The product of one of the most creative and lateral-thinking engineering teams in the British motor industry, it was an indisputedly unique vehicle, combining Land-Rover off-road ability with sufficient comfort for it to be a rewarding road car.

Powered more than adequately by the ex-Buick 3½-liter alloy V8 adopted by Rover in 1967, the car's secret was in the long-travel coil-spring suspension of its beam-axle chassis. With the use of a clever self-levelling strut at the rear, the result was a smooth ride without any compromising of the Land-Rover's unrivalled

rough-terrain capabilities.

    With its crisp and functional styling, it is truly one of the great designs. Even today, more than 20 years on, it has not been beaten in terms of versatility. As a counterpoint to all those short-lived wonder cars of the 1970s, the enduring appeal of the Range-Rover cannot be bettered. Any car that is as at home in a muddy farmyard as parked next to a Countach on the French Riviera has to be something special.

Despite its show car appearance the Lancia Stratos was conceived as a purpose-built rally car, to follow on from the Italian company's successful Fulvia coupés. It proved a dominant presence in 1970s rallying.

Lotus moved upmarket in 1974 with the Elite, a full four-seater powered by the company's first all-Lotus engine. Build quality was uncertain, and the engine in its original form lacked low-down power.

The 1975 replacement for the Lotus Europa was the Esprit, the high-fashion 'folded paper' wedge styled by Giugiaro. This is a late model, a 1984 Turbo.

Two generations of DBS-derived Lagonda: in the foreground is the stretched DBS of which only seven were produced between 1974 and 1976, and behind is the electronics-packed wedge-shaped car that entered production in 1978.

Aston Martin's V8 evolved progressively during the 1970s: this is the 370bhp Vantage version introduced in 1977. It can be recognized by the deep spoiler and the blanked-out grille with inset foglamps.

Porsche's 911 Turbo was announced in 1974. It offered racing car technology with impressive tractability in everyday use. The ultra-wide wheels, heavily flared arches and 'tea tray' spoiler were originally unique to the Turbo, but were subsequently offered on 'regular' Carrera models.

A more modest application of the turbocharging principle: the Saab 99 Turbo. Introduced in 1977, it was a clever way of giving the staid image of the 99 a boost and at the same time moving the marque into more equal contention with the sporting BMWs.

BMW'S first break from convention: the short-lived
M1 mid-engined coupé of 1978-81. Intended for
Group 5 competition, it ended up being used only in
its own M1 race championship.

BMW was highly successful in the European Touring Car championships with the CS coupé, and this led to the lightweight CSL of 1971. Gradually the number of aerodynamic aids on the car grew. Here the silver car displays a deep front spoiler, hood-top 'tabs', a roof spoiler, and the famed 'Batmobile' rear wing.

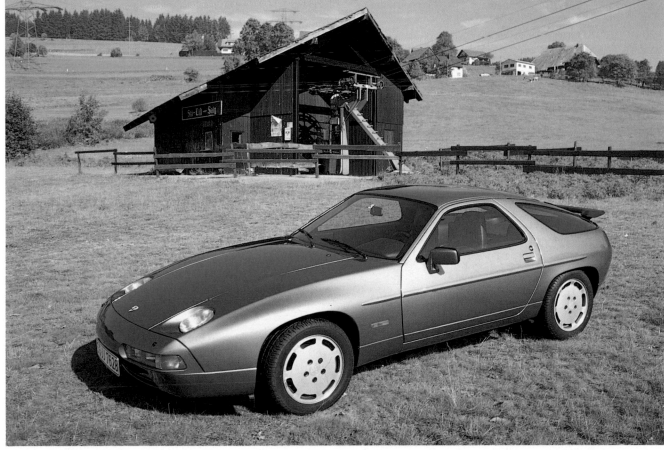

Not quite what Porsche traditionalists expected: the V8-powered 928 launched in 1977. The engine is at the front, the gearbox at the rear, and there is 2 + 2 seating.

New wine in an old bottle.
Jaguar's magical V12 was
premiered in the Series III
E type of 1971, with the longer
2 + 2 wheelbase and identifiable
by its 'birdcage' grille and
flared wheel arches.

The only modern low-priced sports car of the 1970s, the Fiat X1/9. Fiat showed how a transverse front-wheel-drive powerpack could be used to create a practical mid-engined sports car in the Sprite/Midget/Spitfire class. Alas, it cost rather more than these somewhat antiquated designs, and it never received more than token development over the years.

The X1/9 is well-packaged to give good luggage space, so often a weakness of mid-engined designs. There are two trunks, at front and rear, and the spare wheel is mounted behind the passenger seat, alongside the petrol tank.

The right home for the Jaguar V12, and one of the greatest sedans ever made, the Jaguar XJ12: although this is in fact the top Daimler variant, the Daimler Double-Six Vanden Plas.

The replacement for the Rover P6, the SD1, had the misfortune to be launched at a time (1976) when the parent group, BL Cars, was crumbling fast. This obscured the car's very real merits: V8 power, hatchback versatility, well-controlled long-travel suspension using a live rear axle, and well-executed styling by the talented David Bache. This is the high-performance Vitesse version launched in 1982.

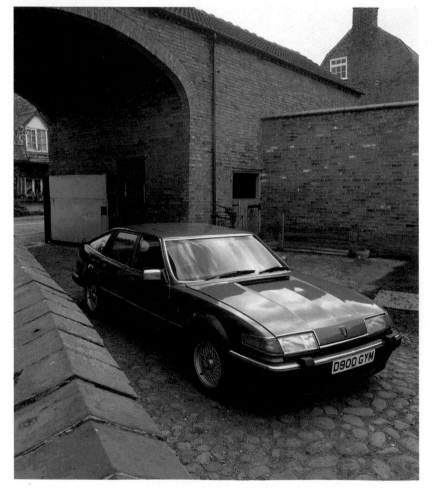

At its 1970 launch there was nothing else like the mould-breaking Range-Rover —
a car with the off-road capabilities and the robustness of the Land-Rover but with
the civilized virtues of a normal road car. Rover was bemused by the way it was
taken up by the fashion-conscious who never strayed off the tarmac.

7

Technology to the Fore

t is arguable that the most significant performance car of the 1980s is nothing more than a modified version of a mass-produced coupé. But if we are talking great cars, then the Audi Quattro has to be the 1980s' most important contribution to the breed. Never mind the more than adequate performance of this German car: its significance is in its permanent four-wheel drive, which has been widely copied ever since.

Introduced in 1980, the Quattro gave the industry a massive and unexpected kick up the pants, and redefined VW subsidiary Audi as a high-tech marque of world stature. Looking back, it all seems so simple: take the Audi coupé, add four-wheel drive from the VW Iltis cross-country vehicle, and install the intercooled turbo engine from the Audi 200 sedan. The result is a light, fast grand tourer with massive reserves of adhesion — and an off-the-shelf rally car of staggering competence.

To keep pace with the rally Quattros, especially in their 450bhp evolved form, rival firms concocted a new breed of rally supercar — 1980s equivalents to the Lancia Stratos. One such was the Ford RS200, a compact 4WD coupé with a mid-mounted 1.8-liter engine. Another was the extraordinary Rover Group Metro 6R4, again mid-engined and with 4WD, but going against the turbo trend by having a normally aspirated V6 engine.

A change in rally regulations rendered such specials obsolete, and the sizeable stocks of Ford RS200s were converted to exciting if somewhat raw road cars; and the Metro 6R4, less amenable to such a transformation, pursued a second career in rallycross.

The Quattro's secret was the compactness and light weight of its straightforward 4WD system. As other car makers followed suit,

Why it was done: rally Audi Quattro in action.

The Audi Quattro of 1980 put four-wheel drive on the agenda for even the most banal family sedans of the 1980s. With its turbocharged five-cylinder 2144cc engine belting out 200bhp, the Quattro, however, was very much the high-performance coupé. This is an example modified by German tuner Walter Treser.

approach, on its Biturbo of 1982, as a way of offering strong performance from a 2-liter V6 engine that fitted under Italian tax thresholds.

The practice is now starting to spread, at least among Japanese manufacturers. Nissan, for instance, has redefined its Z-car as a high-performance sports GT by giving its V6 quad cams and a double-turbo installation. Compared with the previous ungainly boulevard cruiser, the 300ZX has been transformed and with broad-shouldered good looks to match its impressive performance it is now a rival to Porsche. Multi-link front and rear suspension and electronically controlled rear steer complete a seductive package.

Supercars: evolution continues

Meanwhile, the supercar is alive and well, and nowhere more so than at Ferrari, where the flat-12 BB512 Boxer has evolved into the Testarossa. This is a car with Pininfarina styling so flamboyant it is every toy manufacturer and poster company's dream. Do not imagine, however, that those much-imitated side strakes are just for effect: they are used to feed air to the side-mounted radiators that replace the front rad of the previous BB512. With its four-valve cylinder heads, the Testarossa's 5-liter engine develops 390bhp and gives a maximum speed of over 170mph (274km/h).

The Ferrari Testarossa, however, is a big, heavy beast, a car as much for the showman as for the sportsman. For the latter the Italian firm came out in 1987 with a car that took it back to its sports-racing roots: the amazing F40. The last Ferrari designed under the aegis of Enzo Ferrari, it was intended by him to be 'a car which would be a reminder of the great days of Le Mans when you could drive a car on the streets or race it.' Speaking at the F40's launch, he described the car as 'a summary of all the efforts of Ferrari over the years'.

the new technology of viscous couplings and torque-sensing Torsen differentials made modestly priced, compact and ultra-effective all-wheel-drive models a feature of most of the big manufacturers' ranges.

The advance of turbocharging

Another trend of the 1980s was the growth of forced induction: all the firms, it seemed had to have a turbo in their model catalogue. Even Rolls-Royce joined in, and its Bentley Mulsanne Turbo has developed into what many consider the finest sedan in the world, the Mercedes 600 SEL notwithstanding. It was not always so, but suspension modifications have given the latest Turbo R Bentley a degree of chassis poise to match its astonishing and seamless performance.

An interesting variation on the turbo theme is the fitting of twin turbochargers. Maserati was the first company to use this

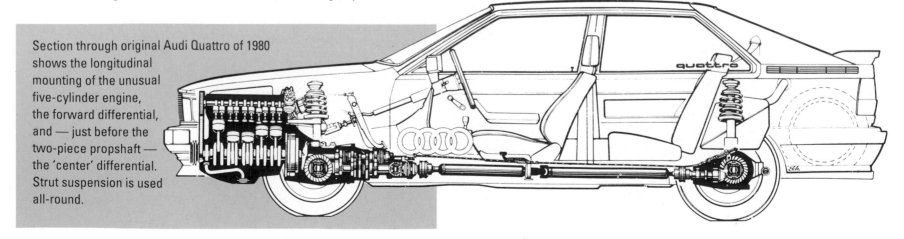

Section through original Audi Quattro of 1980 shows the longitudinal mounting of the unusual five-cylinder engine, the forward differential, and — just before the two-piece propshaft — the 'center' differential. Strut suspension is used all-round.

Ford tried to break back into top-level rallying with the RS200, but the regulations outlawed such cars before the four-wheel drive RS200 had a chance to prove itself. The engine is the twin-cam unit from Ford's previous rally effort, the stillborn rear-drive Escort RS1700T.

of these to be formally launched was a four-turbo V12 of debatable attractiveness carrying the Bugatti name. It remains to be seen how successful this much-ballyhooed enterprise will be.

On a more realistic level, Lotus was another manufacturer to offer a soft-lined revamp of a 1970s favourite. In 1987 this firm restyled the mid-engined Esprit, a car that had gained minor supercar status in 1981 when it became available with a turbo. A less outrageous — and appreciably less costly — machine than the pin-up Italians, the British 2.2-liter is nonetheless capable of 160mph (257km/h) in turbocharged form. Still let down by cut-price detailing, the Esprit Turbo has also been criticized for chassis behaviour that is less than totally convincing; its performance, however, is not in doubt.

Perhaps the biggest supercar surprise of the 1980s was the way Aston Martin's ancient V8, dating to 1967, continued to gain favour, and kept the small British firm of craftsmen sufficiently busy for it to generate the funds to design a replacement.

Few cars have been more eagerly, or more apprehensively, awaited than the new Aston Martin, unveiled in 1988 as the Virage. Styled by much-publicized British duo Ken Greenley and John Heffernan, it manages to be contemporary yet still have an Aston feel, to link it back to such greats as the DB4. Under the skin the car is essentially a refinement of the old machine, but with a sensitively honed chassis and a new 32-valve version of the hand-built all-alloy V8.

The Virage offers a poise and refinement lacking in its

The F40 derived from the 1984 GTO, a homologation special that looked like a boy racer 308GTB but hid a dry-sump twin-turbo V8 mounted longitudinally as opposed to transversely. The F40 carried over this basic configuration, but with the V8's power raised to 478bhp and the engine installed in a Kevlar-reinforced tubular steel chassis. The body was in carbon fibre and Kevlar, and the sparse interior was pure racing car: it did not even have adjustable seats.

Weighing less than 2464lb (1118kg), the F40 offered shattering performance with no compromises to comfort. The stiff suspension filtered nothing out, the steering kicked back every message from the road, and the magnificent engine offered an eruption of wailing power. Demanding, raw, intoxicating and addictive, the F40 was a wonderful last act for Enzo Ferrari.

Over in Sant'Agata, Ferrari's traditional supercar rival Lamborghini carried on until 1990 with its preposterous Countach, but then came out with the smooth-lined but still massively dramatic Diablo. Long and broad, this fat cat extravaganza of a car packs a huge 485bhp thanks to its 5.7-liter V12 with its four valves per cylinder. Essentially it retains the mechanicals of the Countach, will do 0–60mph (0–100km/h) in less than 4 seconds, and is claimed to be good for 202mph (325kph) — although where such speeds can be reached is another matter.

During the last few years such concerns have not stopped a seemingly crazy profusion of projects for 'ultra cars': monster fantasies intended to crack the 200mph (322km/h) barrier. The first

Lancia had devised its own mid-engined rally special, but after the rule changes it turned to turbocharged four-wheel-drive versions of the Delta. The flared arches identify this car as one of these Delta Integrale models.

predecessor, plus enhanced and smoother performance. It deserves better than to have come on stream just as the world economy nose-dived, but with the support of Ford, majority Aston shareholder since 1987, the Virage looks set to flourish in the long term, especially when more potent variants join the range.

Porsche: the rational extravagance?

Another performance car institution is the Porsche 911, first seen in 1963 and still going strong. By the beginning of the 1980s its 'sensible supercar' image was firmly established, thanks to the success of the Turbo.

Continuous uprating culminated in a new 3.2-liter engine in 1983, and an optional 330bhp power unit was introduced for the Turbo two years later. The big image enhancer, though, was the 911-derived 959. It entered production in spring 1987, and only 200 customer cars were made: at a financial loss.

The 959 was intended to be the ultimate 911, and the most complete statement of Porsche's engineering capabilities: it was to be a civilized but multi-purpose supercar, suitable for racing, rallying or blisteringly fast road use. Much of the technology derived from the 956 racers, from which the 959 borrowed its coil-spring rear suspension and a great deal of its power unit detail. The 2850cc flat-six boasted twin-cam four-valve-per-cylinder heads with 956-style water cooling, and there were twin turbochargers, intercooled and plumbed into a comprehensively mapped Bosch Motronic management system. The result was 450bhp, transmitted to all four wheels through a six-speed gearbox. The 4WD featured an automatic torque-splitting mechanism and four selectable programs, and the car's ride height and damping were electronically

The Bentley Mulsanne Turbo was a brave bid to recreate the Bentley mystique. It worked and sales of Bentley-badged versions of the Rolls-Royce soared. As introduced in 1982 the turbocharger saw power of the Rolls V8 boosted from 198bhp to 298bhp, with a near doubling of peak torque.

controlled. Brakes were ABS anti-lock.

Good for nearly 190mph (306km/h), the 959 was a complete contrast to the Ferrari F40: sweet, refined and unintimidating, with a supple ride, low noise levels and a feeling of total security, yet with performance fully the equal of the raw Maranello road racer. The Porsche 959 was a high-profile interlude in the history of the 911, a technological showcase to demonstrate the continuing development potential of the range the company relied on so heavily. The next stage was a 'new' 911, and this arrived in 1989.

Although the more softly contoured bodies looked much as before, the cars were 85 per cent new, said Porsche. Still very much current, the revised models have a twin-plug 3.6-liter engine, modified suspension, power steering, and anti-lock brakes. For the first time, too, there is a four-wheel-drive version, the Carrera 4. The new 911s have been much praised in the press for their balanced and predictable handling, but the favourite seems to be the rear-wheel-drive Carrera 2, for its greater chassis responsiveness.

In contrast to the continuing success of the 911, the big grand-touring 928 failed during the 1980s to win the sales Porsche expected. In compensation, the 924 was developed into the now discontinued 944 and became a benchmark sporting coupé with meaty performance and superbly balanced handling.

The transformation involved fitting a Porsche-designed 2½-liter four-cylinder in place of the 924's VW/Audi power unit, and giving the bodywork a more muscular look inspired by the limited-production 924 Carrera.

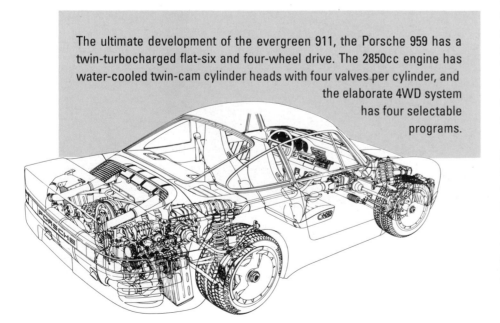

The ultimate development of the evergreen 911, the Porsche 959 has a twin-turbocharged flat-six and four-wheel drive. The 2850cc engine has water-cooled twin-cam cylinder heads with four valves per cylinder, and the elaborate 4WD system has four selectable programs.

Having something in common with the Porsche V8, the new engine was far larger than is normally considered acceptable for a four-cylinder: a four of this size risks being pretty rough. To solve this problem, Porsche adopted a pair of weighted 'balancer' shafts contra-rotating at twice engine speed and countering out-of-balance secondary forces in the engine. Previously used by Mitsubishi, these shafts had been pioneered by Dr Frederick Lanchester (see Chapter 1) at the turn of the century.

In early 1985 a 944 Turbo was introduced, and at the end of the year the original 924 received a slightly downtuned version of the 944's engine. The baby Porsche had grown up in no uncertain fashion, and this process was set to continue. A 16-valve 944 joined the range in 1986. The engine was uprated to 2.7 liters in 1988; that same year the 944 S2 was introduced, with a 3-liter 16-valve engine developing 211bhp. But as the 944's prices spiralled upwards along with its specification, sales fell away, a situation exacerbated by economic recession. Whether the facelifted Porsche 968 will see a revival of fortunes remains to be seen.

Maserati relaunched itself with the Biturbo of 1982, putting big V8s behind it. Variations of the twin-turbocharged V6 have been the company's sole product since then — in various forms, including four-door sedans.

Enter the Japanese

Predictably, the Japanese have now joined the supercar fray. The Honda NSX is intended to be a totally usable supercar, with none of the extravagant impracticalities of the Italian models it seeks to rival, and it has proved a winner. Built around an alloy monocoque and using racing-style forged aluminium suspension components, it has a 24-valve quad-cam 3-liter V6 developing 270bhp. Ingenious features include electronically actuated variable valve timing and a set-up called VVIS (Variable Volume Induction System) to vary the intake manifold flow according to the revs used. Do not look for a distributor, either: each cylinder has its own coil and direct ignition.

The result of all this high-tech is delectably smooth yet urgent power and supremely competent but undemanding roadholding and handling. The Ferrari 348tb may be more inspirational, more emotionally involving, according to the critics, but the Honda has a user-friendliness that makes it utterly practical without being in any way dull.

Below the Honda NSX, the Japanese have established themselves securely in the high-class GT market. The reborn Nissan 300ZX has already been mentioned; countering it is Mazda's RX-7. Unique in having rotary power, it is now in its third generation. More powerful and more sporting than ever, it uses a two-rotor Wankel engine with twin sequential turbochargers — as on the Porsche 959. This means that one turbo operates at low to medium revs, cutting in more quickly than normal, and then the second turbo steps in at higher revs to provide full boost. The result is a more even power delivery than with an ordinary turbo system. There is also a new chassis with double-wishbone suspension all round; and despite a 20 per cent increase in body stiffness, the latest Mazda RX-7 is a full 200lb (91kg) lighter than its predecessor.

A few years ago the condescending Westerner would never have expected such technical prowess from the Japanese. Today, however, it is Japan that is making the running. This was made abundantly clear when Toyota launched its Lexus LS400 in 1989. For the first time cars such as Jaguar and Mercedes were being targeted, and the Lexus soon showed it did not have to apologize to either marque.

The silky-smooth quad-cam V8 is one of the best mass-production power units in the world, and the rest of the car has refinement to match. Admittedly the

The Z-car is back, with a vengeance. While the smaller 200ZX has slotted neatly into the market position of the original 1969 240Z, Nissan has created a worthy Porsche rival in the twin-turbo 300ZX.

A sports car revival?

Let us end on a more positive note. As the 20th century draws to a close one of the most life-giving forms of motoring is undergoing a revival: the sports car is returning.

For years the choice of open two-seaters has been limited: a handful of British specialist makes, a few European antiquities such as the Alfa Spyder and Fiat X1/9, and the odd high-priced cruiser such as the Mercedes-Benz SL and, from America, the Chevrolet Corvette. The glory days of MGs, Triumphs, and sporting open Jaguars seemed part of history.

It took Mazda to break the ice, in 1989, and to have the courage to produce an affordable two-seater. Studying in detail all the most-loved European sports cars, the Japanese firm's Californian design studio carried out an inspired 'pick and mix' exercise that blended characteristics of everything from the original Lotus Elan to the Alfa Spyder — but with up-to-date Mazda mechanicals. Traditionalists find the resultant MX-5 a little pasteurized: but is that not just another way of saying it is a modern car rather than a crude throwback to a less technically-enlightened era?

In the United States the Mazda sells for the sort of money that would have bought an MGB in the old days, and its runaway success has prompted the Rover Group, holders of the MG name, at last to get under way a new MG for the 1990s.

Meanwhile, the Japanese are not standing still, and Suzuki has now launched its own similarly sized sports car, the Cappuccino, and Daihatsu looks set to follow. Then there is the Honda Beat, a mid-engined 660cc screamer that is spoken of as a modern-day Austin-Healey Sprite.

In Britain, Lotus has revived the Elan name for one of the longest-awaited new products in the business, a high-price two-seater that goes against received sports car wisdom by having front-wheel drive. To give the desired handling the Elan, launched in 1989, uses a patented 'interactive wishbone' system at the front. Expressed simply, this mounts the inner wishbone pick-ups on a separate alloy 'raft' each side rather than directly on to the chassis. The 'raft' is then mounted to the chassis to give carefully controlled compliance, allowing the actual wishbone pivots to be very stiffly bushed to retain accurate wheel control. As a consequence, the Elan handles precisely, and without the torque steer expected of a front-wheel-drive design. Such engineering enables Lotus to claim to have created a sports car that takes design forward rather than one that merely restates and refines the technology of the 1970s.

The same could be said of another invigorating sports car of the 1980s: the limited-production BMW Z1 of 1989–91. The Z1 had the good fortune to be born without design constraints, as a rolling showcase for the BMW think-tank, the *Technik* division. Thus the

exterior styling does not quite make the grade, and the interior lacks the studied opulence of some European rivals, but the quality of Lexus engineering is incontestable.

Continental manufacturers are fighting hard to meet the challenge, and the latest S class Mercedes-Benz in its top V12 form is an awesome statement of German technology. The 6-liter engine boasts everything from an electronic anti-knock device for each cylinder to what is claimed to be the most advanced engine management system in the world. The windows are double-glazed. The trunk and doors are self-closing. The heating system works for 20 minutes after the engine has been switched off. Electrical assists are everywhere.

However, the 17ft (5.2m) Mercedes weighs 5070lb (2300kg) — more than three times a Citroën AX supermini — and costs almost as much as a Rolls-Royce. BMW's 4222lb (1915kg) V12 750iL seems almost modest in comparison.The 600 has super-strong and effortless performance, nimble cornering that belies the car's size, and all the quiet excellence in other areas that you would expect from a top Mercedes. But is this the sort of no-compromise leviathan the motor industry should be producing in the ethically aware 1990s?

Enzo Ferrari's last car design, the F40. Seen in the perspective of the firm's history, the F40 was in fact a spiritual descendant of the 1950s Ferrari you could run around town with during the week and race at weekends.

designers could apply daring engineering solutions that in a more mainstream product would inevitably have been diluted.

Built around a zinc-coated steel hull, the BMW Z1 has a bonded-in plastic composites floorpan and thermoplastic body panels that can be put on or taken off in 30 minutes. As if this were not enough, there are sliding doors that disappear into the deep sills at the press of a button, enabling true open-air motoring.

The taut, compact styling hides a further surprise: the Z1's

aerodynamics are excellent for an open car, and are the result of many subtle touches. These include a concave hood that acts as a front spoiler, and a silencer that has an aerofoil profile to aid air flow under the car.

The extravagant engineering of cars such as the Lamborghini Diablo and the Mercedes 600SEL are splendid statements of the late 20th century's command of automotive engineering. But if the innovative technology of the Lotus Elan and the BMW Z1 can be applied to small, lightweight and affordably priced sports cars, the great cars of the 1990s could be the most exciting and approachable for many a decade.

The Ferrari GTO of 1984-5: it might look like a kind of 308GTB, but the longitudinal mounting of the V8 meant the wheelbase was longer and the rear overhang shorter. The body used fiberglass and plastic composites to reduce weight, and the running gear drew on racing technology.

The Ferrari 308 evolved into the 328, gaining a 32-valve head on the way, and continued to be available as both a closed coupé and as a GTS spyder. A 2-liter 208 was available for the Italian market, and from 1982 could be had with a turbocharger. This is a 328GTB.

The optional wing adds to the drama of later Lamborghini Countach models: this is a 198x *quattrovalvole*.

Replacing the Countach was a hard act, but the Diablo of 1990 fully met expectations. The styling is by Marcello Gandini, who was responsible for the Miura while at Bertone.

Virage: the first properly new Aston Martin product since 1967. Under its alloy skin the Virage retains a De Dion rear axle, but considerably lightened. The V8 engine has been heavily revised and in its new 32-valve form develops 330bhp.

Lotus carried out an in-house restyling of the Giugiaro original
to relaunch the Esprit in 1987. This is the turbo version, which in
its latest charge-cooled form developed 264bhp.

Porsche's amazing 959, versatile enough to be a road car, a rally winner, or a successful racer. The body makes extensive use of the latest plastics, and the engine has water-cooled four-valve heads, twin intercooled turbochargers, and a power output of 450bhp.

The Porsche 911 continued to evolve throughout the 1980s. This 1985 car is a Carrera SE (Sports Equipment), with Turbo body and suspension but a normally aspirated 3.2-liter engine.

The 911 entered the 1990s in a new format, with a restyled
body hiding all-coil suspension, power-assisted steering,
twin-plug 3.6-liter power, and the option of four-wheel drive.
A Tiptronic automatic gearbox is also available.

From humble beginnings as the 924 parts-bin special, the 'cheap' Porsche was pushed relentlessly upmarket. This 944 Turbo from 1986 has a 220bhp engine of 2479cc. While this capacity was always retained for the Turbo, the size of the normally aspirated 944 engine had climbed to 2990cc by 1988.

Honda's mid-engined NSX is a real rival to Europe's best, and draws on racing practice for its advanced engineering. It is largely hand-built in its own special factory. The transversely set V6 is not turbocharged, and develops 270bhp.

Mazda announced its third-generation rotary-engined RX-7 in 1991. A
concerted effort to save weight has led to the 255bhp twin-turbo two-seater
being a full 672lb (305kg) lighter than the Nissan 300ZX.

The styling might be clumsy, but Toyota's Lexus LS400 is a genuine rival to the top models from Europe. The 4-liter quad-cam V8 delivers 241bhp and has superlative refinement, and the double-wishbone suspension all-round gives exemplary roadholding, handling and ride. Here the Lexus is shown with a Series III Daimler Double-Six.

Mercedes wants its new S class in its V12 6-liter form to be the best car in the world; lesser variants use a 3.2-liter straight-six or a V8 in 4.2-liter or 5-liter form. Despite their size and weight, the cars handle as if they were much smaller, and the standards they set in all areas are extraordinarily high.

The ultra-neat presentation of the Mercedes 600SEL's V12 power unit, which develops 408bhp and a massive 427lb ft of torque. It has four valves per cylinder and two cams per bank.

In 1989 Mercedes replaced its long in the tooth second-generation SL with a new model. Power remained either straight-six or V8, but the six is available in either 12- or 24-valve form and the V8 is now a 326bhp quad-cam unit. A roll bar rises automatically if electronic sensors indicate an accident, real or imminent.

The Jaguar XJ-S was launched in 1975, and is built on the old XJ6 floorpan in its original short-wheelbase form. Much improved over the years, it is still handicapped by appalling packaging. In 1991 the XJ-S was lightly restyled, and this is the V12 coupé version. A cabriolet is also available, and the 4-liter AJ6 six-cylinder engine is an alternative to the V12.

The ultimate no-compromise sports car: the Caterham Seven. Back in 1973 Caterham took over manufacture of the Lotus Seven, and since then the small company has steadily developed the design. It is now structurally much stronger, has a supple De Dion rear, and is built to first-rate standards. It has shattering acceleration, and roadholding and handling without equal. This is the latest version, with a catalyst-equipped Rover Group 1.4-liter engine.

After two decades of unforgivable management inertia the former British Leyland — now the Rover Group — reintroduced the Mini-Cooper in 1990. The 1275cc 'New Cooper' now takes the lion's share of Mini sales, and in its latest form boasts fuel-injection to meet emission regulations.

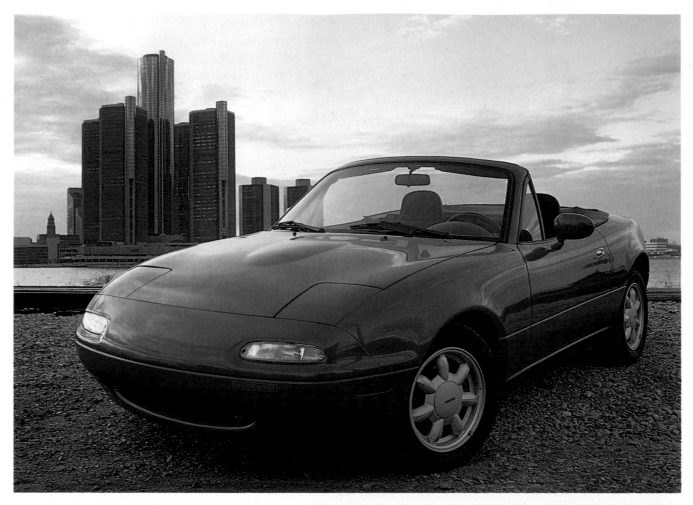

May familiarity never breed contempt — because Mazda's MX-5 had the Japanese doing what everyone else was just talking about, and reviving the 'traditional' sports car. It is an instant classic. The 1598cc twin-cam drives the rear wheels, and suspension is double-wishbone back and front.

The sports car initiative has passed to Japan. The Honda Beat is everything a 1990s Sprite should be. The mid-engined 660cc three-cylinder has four valves per cylinder and pushes out 64bhp. The dynamics are superb but sales are restricted to Japan.

GREAT CARS OF THE WORLD

Short and stubby, the Lotus Elan launched in 1989 has front-wheel drive: a controversial decision, but the suspension geometry is very special. Power comes from an Isuzu twin-cam of 1588cc in either 130bhp normally aspirated form or as a 165bhp turbocharged SE.

Lighter, roomier and more aerodynamically efficient, the new Chevrolet Corvette introduced in 1983 was built around an aluminium spine and used a single fiberglass transverse rear spring for the independent rear suspension.

Wilder than the wildest, and just screaming
power, the Dodge Viper has been actively
promoted by Carroll Shelby as a Cobra
for the 1990s. Power comes from a 400bhp
8-liter V10 planting down a massive 450lb ft
of torque through a six-speed gearbox.

BMW's replacement for the 6 series coupé is the 850i, powered by the V12 first seen in the 750i sedan. The 300bhp 5-liter gives the BMW 160mph (257km/h) performance, but the car is more grand tourer than sports car.

A brave departure: BMW's first sports car since the 507 of the fifties, the thermoplastics-panelled Z1 bristles with innovative features and has a superb chassis. A major attention-grabber is the sliding doors that disappear into the broad sills of the steel hull.

BIBLIOGRAPHY

This bibliography is not comprehensive, but gives a selection of the most useful books for further reading. Exclusion of a title should not be seen as implying any judgement on that particular book's worth. Not all titles are currently in print, but most of those listed should be obtainable without difficulty from established motoring bookshops

AC
McLellan, John: *The Classic ACs*, MRP
Mills, Rinsey: *Original AC Ace & Cobra*, Bay View Books

ALFA ROMEO
Borgeson, Griffith: *The Alfa Romeo Tradition*, Haynes
Cherrett, Angela: *Alfa Romeo Tipo 6C*, Haynes
Hull, Peter and Slater, Roy: *Alfa Romeo*, Transport Bookman Publications
Owen, David: *The Alfasud*, MRP

ALVIS
Day, Kenneth: *Alvis — The Story of the Red Triangle*, Haynes

ASTON MARTIN & LAGONDA
Bowler, Michael: *Aston Martin V8*, Cadogan Publications
Chudecki, Paul: *The Aston Martin and Lagonda (V8 models from 1970)*, MRP
Whyte, Andrew: *The Aston Martin and Lagonda (six-cylinder DBs)*, MRP

AUDI
Henry, Alan: *Audi Quattro*, Cadogan

AUSTIN
Wyatt, R J : *The Austin Seven — The Motor for the Million*, David & Charles

AUSTIN-HEALEY
Clausager, Anders Ditlev: *Original Austin-Healey*, Bay View Books
Dymock, Eric: *The Sprites and Midgets*, MRP
Healey, Geoffrey: *Austin-Healey — The Story of the Big Healeys*, Gentry/Haynes
Healey, Geoffrey: *Austin-Healey — Frogeyes, Sprites and Midgets*, Gentry/Haynes

BENTLEY
Ellman-Brown, Michael: *Bentley — The Silent Sports Car*, Dalton Watson
Frostick, Michael: *From Cricklewood to Crewe*, Dalton Watson
Hay, Michael: *Bentley — The Vintage Years, 1919-31*, Dalton Watson
Hay, Michael: *Bentley 4½-litre Supercharged*, Haynes
Steel, Rodney: *Bentley — The Cars from Crewe*, Dalton Watson

BMW
Schrader, Halwart and Wakefield, Ron : *BMW — A History*, Osprey

BRISTOL
Oxley, Charles : *Bristol — An Illustrated History*, Crowood

BUGATTI
Borgeson, Griffith: *Bugatti by Borgeson*, Haynes
Conway, Hugh: *Bugatti — le pur-sang des automobiles*, Haynes

CADILLAC
Hendry, Maurice: *Cadillac — Standard of the World*, Automobile Quarterly
McCall, Walter MP: *80 Years of Cadillac / La Salle*, Crestline

CHEVROLET
Langworth, Richard: *The Corvettes, 1953-88*, MRP
Ludvigsen, Karl: *Corvette — America's Star-spangled Sports Car*, Automobile Quarterly

CITROËN
Sabates, Fabien: *Citroën 2CV vu par la presse*, Collection Auto Archives
de Serres, Olivier: *Le Grand Livre Citroën*, EPA
de Serres, Olivier: *Le Grand Livre de la Traction Avant*, EPA
Taylor, James: *The Citroën 2CV and derivatives*, MRP

DAIMLER AND LANCHESTER
Freeman, Tony: *Daimler and Lanchester — An Illustrated History*, Academy
Smith, Brian: *The Daimler Tradition*, Transport Bookman Publications

DATSUN
Hutton, Ray: *The 'Z' Series Datsuns*, MRP

DE TOMASO
Wyss, Wallace A: *De Tomaso Automobiles*, Osprey

FACEL-VEGA
Daninos, Jean: *Facel-Vega*, EPA

FERRARI
Curtis, Anthony: *Ferrari Dino*, Crowood
Gross, Ken: *Ferrari 250GT swb*, Osprey
Henry, Alan: *The Ferrari Dino 246, 308 and 328*, MRP
Nichols, Mel: *Ferrari Berlinetta Boxer*, Osprey
Owen, David: *Ferrari four-seaters*, Osprey
Prunet, Antoine: *Ferrari — The Road Cars*, Haynes
Tanner, Hans (with Doug Nye): *Ferrari*, Haynes
Thompson, Jonathan: *Ferrari Cabriolets and Spyders*, Osprey
Webb, Ian: *Ferrari Dino 206GT, 246GT & GTS*, Osprey
Willoughby, Geoff: *Ferrari 308 and Mondial*, Osprey

FORD
Langworth, Richard: *The Mustangs, 1964-73*, MRP
Witzenburg, Gary: *Mustang!*, Automobile Quarterly

FRAZER NASH
Jenkinson, Denis S : *From Chain-Drive to Turbocharger*, PSL
Thirlby, David: *The Chain-Drive Frazer Nash*, MacDonald

ISOTTA-FRASCHINI
Anselmi, Angelo Tito: *Isotta-Fraschini*, Milani
Nicholson, Tim: *Isotta-Fraschini — The Noble Pride of Italy*, Ballantines

JAGUAR
Porter, Philip: *Original Jaguar E-Type*, Bay View Books
Porter, Philip: *Original Jaguar XK*, Bay View Books
Porter, Philip: *Jaguar E-Type — The Definitive History*, Haynes
Skilleter, Paul: *Jaguar Saloon Cars*, (Haynes)
Skilleter, Paul: *Jaguar Sports Cars*, Haynes
Skilleter, Paul: *The XJ Series*, MRP
Thorley, Nigel: *Jaguar Mk I and Mk II Saloons*, Bay View Books
Whyte, Andrew: *Jaguar — The Definitive History of a Great British Car*, PSL

JEEP
Ackerson, Robert C: *Jeep — The 50 Year History*, Haynes
Jeudy, Jean-Gabriel and Tavarine, Marc: *The Jeep*, Haynes

JENSEN
Anderson, Keith: *Jensen*, Haynes
Taylor, Mike: *Jensen Interceptor*, Haynes

JOWETT
Clark, Paul and Nankivell, Edmund: *The Complete Jowett History*, Foulis

LAGONDA
Seaton, Geoffrey: *Lagonda — An Illustrated History 1900-1950*, Crowood

LAMBORGHINI
Box, Rob de la Rive and Crump, Richard: *Lamborghini — The Cars from Sant'Agata Bolognese*, Osprey
Lyons, Pete: *The Complete Book of Lamborghini*, Haynes
Marchet, Jean-François and Coltrin, Pierre: *Lamborghini Countach*, Osprey
Marchet, Jean-François: *Lamborghini Espada and the 4-seaters*, Osprey
Marchet, Jean-François; *Lamborghini Urraco and the V8s*, Osprey

LANCHESTER
Freeman, Tony; Long, Brian; Hood, Chris (ed): *Lanchester Cars*, Academy

LANCIA
Trow, Nigel: *Lancia Stratos*, Osprey
Weernink, Wim Oude: *La Lancia*, MRP

LAND-ROVER
Taylor, James: *The Land-Rover 1948-88*, Motor Racing Publications

LINCOLN
Dammann, Geo H and Wagner, James K: *The Cars of Lincoln Mercury*, Crestline

LOTUS
Bolster, John V: *The Elan and Europa*, MRP
Coulter, Jeremy: *The Lotus and Caterham Sevens*, MRP
Ortenburger, Dennis E: *The Lotus Elite*, PSL
Robson, Graham: *The Third-Generation Lotuses — Elite, Eclat, Esprit, Excel*, MRP

MASERATI
Box, Rob de la Rive and Crump, Richard: *Maserati Road Cars*, Osprey

MAYBACH
Metternich, Michael Graf Wolff: *Maybach*, Uhle & Kleimann

MERCEDES-BENZ
Steinwedel, Louis William: *The Mercedes-Benz Story*, Chilton
Taylor, James: *Mercedes-Benz since 1945, Vols 1-3*, MRP

MG
Clausager, Anders Ditlev: *Original MG T-Series*, Bay View Books
McComb, Wilson: *MG by McComb*, Osprey
Robson, Graham: *The MGA, MGB & MGC*, Motor Racing Publications
Robson, Graham; *The T-Series MGs*, Motor Racing Publications

MINI
Brigden, John: *The Sporting Minis*, Motor Racing Publications
Golding, Rob: *Mini after 30 years*, Osprey
Pomeroy, Laurence: *The Mini Story*, Temple Press

MORRIS
Jarman, Lytton P and Barraclough, Robin: *The Bullnose and Flatnose Morris*, David & Charles
Skilleter, Paul: *Morris Minor — The World's Supreme Small Car*, Osprey

MORGAN
Houston Bowden, Gregory: *Morgan*, Osprey

PACKARD
Turnquist, Robert E: *The Packard Story*, Barnes

PANHARD
Parot, Benoit: *Panhard — la doyenne d'avant garde*, EPA

PORSCHE
Cotton, Michael: *Porsche Progress*, PSL
Cotton, Michael: *Porsche 911 Turbo*, Osprey
Cotton, Michael: *Porsche 924 and 944*, Motor Racing
    Publications
Frere, Paul: *Porsche 911 Story*, PSL
Frere, Paul: *Porsche 911*, EPA
Jenkinson, Denis J: *Porsche 356*, Osprey
Lewandowski, Jürgen: *Porsche 959*, Christophorus
Sloniger, Jerry: *Porsche 924/928/944*, Osprey

RANGE-ROVER
Taylor, James: *The Range-Rover*, MRP

RILEY
Styles, David G : *Sporting Rileys — The Forgotten Champions*,
    Dalton Watson

ROLLS-ROYCE
Bird, Anthony and Hallows, Ian: *The Rolls-Royce Motor Car*,
    Batsford
Dalton, Lawrence: *Those Elegant Rolls-Royces*, Dalton Watson
Dalton, Lawrence: *Rolls-Royce, the Classic Elegance*, Dalton
    Watson
Fasal, John: *The Rolls-Royce Twenty*, Burgess
Gentile, Raymond: *The Rolls-Royce Phantom II Continental*,
    Dalton Watson
Robson, Graham: *The Rolls-Royce & Bentley*, Vols 1-3, MRP
Schrader, Halwart: *Rolls-Royce Cars*, Nishen

ROVER
Robson, Graham: *The Rover Story*, PSL
Taylor, James: *The Classic Rovers*, MRP

SUNBEAM
Taylor, Mike: *Tiger — The Making of a Sports Car*, Haynes

TALBOT-LAGO
Spitz, Alain: *Talbot — des Talbot-Darracq aux Talbot-Lago*, EPA

TRIUMPH
Piggott, Bill: *Original Triumph TR*, Bay View Books
Robson, Graham: *The Triumph TRs*, MRP

VOLKSWAGEN
Etzold, Hans Rudiger (ed): *The Beetle — The Chronicles of the
    People's Car*, Vols 1-3, Haynes
Wood, Jonathan: *The Volkswagen Beetle*, MRP

GENERAL
There are countless more general books, of varying depth. The
most informative, however, are generally out-of-print titles from
the first post-war generation of motoring historians. The books
listed in this section need not be hard to find, and are written
by some of the best-known names in the field.

Bird, Anthony: *The Motor Car, 1765-1914*, Batsford
Bolster, John V. *The Upper Crust*, Weidenfeld & Nicolson
Clutton, Cecil and Stanford, John: *The Vintage Motor Car*,
    Batsford
Nicholson, T R: *The Vintage Car*, Batsford
Scott-Moncrieff, David: *Veteran and Edwardian Motor Cars*,
    Batsford
Sedgwick, Michael, *Cars of the 1930s*, Batsford
Sedgwick, Michael: *The Motor Car 1946-56*, Batsford

This bibliography was compiled with the kind help of leading
motoring bookshop Chaters', who can supply most of the titles
listed, including many of those currently out of print. Chater'
Motoring Booksellers is at 8 South Street, Isleworth, Middlesex
TW7 7BG (tel: 081-568 9750 / 081-560 2666 / fax: 081-569 8273)

INDEX

figures in italics denote photographs

ACKNOWLEDGEMENTS

Most of the photographs illustrating this book come from the Haymarket Magazines motoring photo library and are mainly drawn from the files of *Classic and Sportscar* and *Autocar & Motor* magazines. The photographers responsible are: Tim Andrew, Matt Barnes, Jeff Bloxham, Peter Burn, John Colley, Paul Debois, Mel Dew, David Goldman, Julian Mackie, James Mann, Mike McCarthy, 'Moni', Andrew Morland, Stan Papior, Peter Robain, Phil Rudge, Mike Valente, Mick Walsh and Andrew Yeadon. My apologies if I have left out anyone's name.

Grateful thanks also to Nick Georgano for providing photos, to David Sewell at the Bugatti Owners' Club, to Sara Hoskins at Mercedes-Benz, and to Barry Littlewood of the Museum of British Road Transport in Coventry for providing the photo of the museum's Maudslay.

A big 'thank you' is also owed to designer Kelly Maskall for putting it all together, and to my editor at *Classic and Sportscar*, Giles Chapman, for his tolerance of my erratic work-pattern while the book was being written. Finally, thanks to Julie Lawrence for keeping me sane during this period.